FINAL DRAFT

2

DRAFT

Teacher's Manual

Series Editor: **Jeanne Lambert**
The New School

Jill Bauer
North Seattle College
Mike S. Boyle
Sara Stapleton
North Seattle College

with
Wendy Asplin, University of Washington
and
Jane Stanley McGrath

CAMBRIDGE
UNIVERSITY PRESS

CAMBRIDGE
UNIVERSITY PRESS

32 Avenue of the Americas, New York NY 10013-2473, USA

Cambridge University Press is part of the University of Cambridge.

It furthers the University's mission by disseminating knowledge in the pursuit of education, learning and research at the highest international levels of excellence.

www.cambridge.org
Information on this title: www.cambridge.org/9781107495425

First published 2016

Printed in Mexico by Editorial Impresora Apolo, S.A. de C.V.

A catalog record for this publication is available from the British Library.

ISBN 978-1-107-49539-5 Student's Book Level 2
ISBN 978-1-107-49541-8 Student's Book with Writing Skills Interactive Level 2
ISBN 978-1-107-49542-5 Teacher's Manual Level 2

Additional resources for this publication at www.cambridge.org/finaldraft

Cambridge University Press has no responsibility for the persistence or accuracy of URLs for external or third-party Internet Web sites referred to in this publication and does not guarantee that any content on such Web sites is, or will remain, accurate or appropriate. Information regarding prices, travel timetables, and other factual information given in this work is correct at the time of first printing but Cambridge University Press does not guarantee the accuracy of such information thereafter.

Art direction, book design, and photo research: emc design limited
Layout services: emc design limited

CONTENTS

INTRODUCTION

Final Draft *is a four-level academic writing series for high beginning / low intermediate- to high advanced-level students of North American English.* The series prepares students to write in a college or university setting by focusing on the topics, rhetorical modes, skills, vocabulary, and grammar necessary for students to develop their academic writing. Students are given the tools to master academic writing. First, they learn and practice foundational academic writing skills essential to writing paragraphs and essays. Then, following a process-based approach, students move through the writing process, from brainstorming with graphic organizers to organizing and developing their ideas with outlines, before completing the final draft of their unit assignment.

Final Draft *provides frequent and realistic writing models.* Each unit features writing models that reinforce the concept that writing is purposeful. The Writing in the Real World article engages students and introduces them to the topic, ideas, language, and elements of structure or rhetorical mode taught in the unit. The Student Model then demonstrates the conventions of the target structure and mode. This progression from authentic text to traditional academic writing helps students new to academic discourse first understand the purpose of communicating with a given mode before turning their attention to mastering the form.

Final Draft *focuses on key academic vocabulary.* Students need to encounter high-frequency academic vocabulary and learn how to use it naturally in preparation for college-level writing. The academic phrases and collocations in the series were selected based on the findings of research into the *Cambridge English Corpus*. Analysis of this multibillion-word collection of real-life English indicates the language that is most relevant for academic writing, with a focus here on longer lexical chunks. The academic vocabulary in the series is also corpus-informed, the majority of words coming from Averil Coxhead's Academic Word List (AWL) and the remaining items taken from Michael West's General Service List (GSL). AWL words are identified as such in the index of the student's book.

Vocabulary items are contextualized and recycled throughout the unit. Academic collocations or academic phrases are introduced and practiced in alternating units. The writing models recycle these words and phrases in academic contexts, and in the final section of each unit students are prompted to find places where they can use these vocabulary items naturally when writing their end-of-unit assignment.

The grammar presented in **Final Draft** *is corpus-informed.* Corpus research tells us the most common grammar mistakes for specific grammar points in academic writing. Students study the most common grammar mistakes drawn from the *Cambridge Learner Corpus*, a unique collection of over 50 million examples of nonnative speakers' writing. Students then work to repair them in editing activities. At the end of the unit, students are reminded to correct these mistakes as they write their assignment, which helps promote accuracy in their writing.

Final Draft *teaches students to understand and avoid plagiarism.* The series provides a robust presentation of techniques for understanding and avoiding plagiarism. Each unit includes an overview of a common plagiarism-related issue, along with a skill-building activity. This innovative approach is pedagogical, not punitive. Many ESL students struggle with a range of issues related to plagiarism. By including realistic examples and practical activities in each unit, *Final Draft* helps students avoid plagiarism and improve their academic writing.

Writing Skills Interactive *provides extra practice in key writing skills.* This online course, which can be purchased with *Final Draft*, provides graduated instruction and practice in key writing skills to help students build confidence and fluency. Each unit provides an animated presentation of the target writing skill, along with automatically graded practice activities. Each unit closes with a quiz so students can assess their progress.

Special Sections

YOUR TURN ACTIVITIES

Each unit includes a wide variety of regular writing practice activities, including Your Turn activities which ask students to go beyond traditional practice to apply the skills, ideas, and language they have learned to their selected writing prompt. As a result, by the time they write their end-of-unit assignment, they are thoroughly prepared for the writing process because they have already practiced relevant skills and generated useful ideas and language to incorporate into their work. This makes the writing process less daunting than it would otherwise be.

Series Levels

Level	Description	CEFR Levels
Final Draft 1	Low Intermediate	A2
Final Draft 2	Intermediate	B1
Final Draft 3	High Intermediate	B2
Final Draft 4	Advanced	C1

Additional teacher resources for each level are available online at cambridge.org/finaldraft.

Final Draft 2

This book is designed for a semester-long writing course. There is enough material in the student's book for a course of 50 to 70 class hours. The number of class hours will vary, depending on how much of a unit is assigned outside of class and how much time a teacher decides to spend on specific elements in class. Because units are carefully designed to build toward the final writing activity, teachers are encouraged to work through each unit in chronological order. However, units can generally stand alone, so teachers can teach them in the order that best suits their needs.

Unit Overview and Teaching Suggestions

UNIT OPENER

Purpose

- To introduce the unit topic and academic discipline in an engaging way
- To elicit preliminary thinking about the unit theme and structure or rhetorical mode

Teaching Suggestion

Have students respond to the quote in writing by freewriting their ideas or by agreeing or disagreeing with the central message of the quote.

1 PREPARE YOUR IDEAS

In Section 1, students begin to explore the unit structure or rhetorical mode and choose their writing prompt for the unit.

A Connect to Academic Writing

Purpose

- To introduce the unit structure or rhetorical mode in an accessible way
- To connect academic writing to students' lives and experience

Teaching Suggestion

To deepen the conversation, elicit additional examples from students of how the rhetorical mode connects to thinking they already do in their lives.

B Reflect on the Topic

Purpose

- To show a writing prompt that elicits the rhetorical mode
- To introduce an appropriate graphic organizer for brainstorming and organizing ideas for the mode
- To choose a prompt for the unit writing assignment and begin generating ideas for the topic
- To engage students with the writing process early in the unit

Teaching Suggestion

Group students together who chose the same writing prompt and have them brainstorm ideas for the topic. Groups can then share their ideas with the class and receive immediate feedback.

2 EXPAND YOUR KNOWLEDGE

In Section 2, students learn academic vocabulary and read a real-world text that contains elements of the unit structure or rhetorical mode.

Ⓐ Academic Vocabulary

Purpose

- To introduce high-frequency academic words from the Academic Word List and the General Service List
- To focus on the meaning of the target vocabulary within a thematic context

Teaching Suggestion

Have students choose vocabulary words from the activity that they still have trouble understanding or contextualizing and write sentences using them. They can share their sentences in groups or with the class and receive immediate feedback.

Ⓑ Academic Collocations / Academic Phrases

Purpose

- To teach academic collocations and phrases that frequently occur in academic reading and writing
- To encourage the use of language chunks that will make student writing more natural and academic
- To tie academic vocabulary to the unit theme

Teaching Suggestion

Have students use the Internet to find more authentic examples of the collocations in sentences as a homework assignment. Students can then share their examples with the class or in groups.

Ⓒ Writing in the Real World

Purpose

- To provide authentic content, ideas, and language in a context related to the unit theme
- To introduce elements of the unit rhetorical mode in an authentic reading
- To recycle new academic vocabulary and collocations or phrases
- To introduce features of the unit structure or mode

Teaching Suggestion

After students have read and understood the text, assign a paragraph or section to small groups, and have students work together to explain the purpose of each sentence in the section. Sample student responses: *The first sentence <u>introduces</u> the topic, the second and third sentences <u>give background information</u> on the topic,* etc.

3 STUDY ACADEMIC WRITING

In Section 3, students read and analyze a student model of a traditional academic paragraph or essay. A detailed examination of elements of the unit structure or rhetorical mode follows.

Ⓐ Student Model

Purpose

- To provide an aspirational student model for the unit structure or rhetorical mode
- To deepen understanding of writing technique through real-time analysis
- To provide a context for writing skills that will be studied in Section 4
- To familiarize students with writing prompts that can be answered using the unit mode
- To recycle academic vocabulary and collocations or phrases
- To evaluate and generate more ideas on the unit theme
- To demonstrate the organization and development of ideas in traditional academic writing

Teaching Suggestion

In small groups, have students discuss their answers to the Analyze Writing Skills tasks. Then have each group present to the class on something they noticed that they found interesting or still have questions about. This offers an opportunity to deepen the discussion on writing technique.

Ⓑ Unit Structure or Rhetorical Mode

Purpose

- To deepen understanding of the unit structure or rhetorical mode
- To explain key elements of the unit structure or rhetorical mode
- To have students practice writing elements of a paragraph or essay

Teaching Suggestion

Following the activities in this section in chronological order will ensure that students have covered all the key features of the unit structure or rhetorical mode. However, if students need less work in some areas, you may want to skip those parts in class and assign the activities for homework.

In general, practice activities, including Your Turn activities, can be completed in class and immediate feedback can be given by peers or the instructor. Alternately, these sections can be assigned as homework and brought to class for review.

4 SHARPEN YOUR SKILLS

In Section 4, students review and practice key writing skills, specific applications of grammar for writing, and ways to avoid plagiarism.

A Writing Skill

Purpose

- To provide practice with discrete writing skills that students can apply to their unit writing assignments
- To deepen knowledge of rhetorical strategies

Teaching Suggestion

Collect writing samples from one or more of the Your Turn activities in this section. Reproduce several for the class – on the board, as handouts, on a screen – to use as an editing activity.

B Grammar for Writing

Purpose

- To present specific applications of grammar for academic writing
- To draw attention to the most common grammar mistakes made by students
- To promote grammatical accuracy in academic writing
- To improve students' editorial skills

Teaching Suggestion

After students complete the editing task at the end of the section, have students identify elements of the unit mode (e.g., language, structure) and parts of an academic paragraph (e.g., topic sentence, examples, other supporting details).

C Avoiding Plagiarism

Purpose

- To increase awareness of the issues surrounding plagiarism
- To build skills and strategies for avoiding plagiarism
- To provide regular practice of writing skills useful for avoiding plagiarism

Teaching Suggestion

Have one student read the student question in the Q & A aloud; all other students should listen with their books closed. Elicit possible responses from the class and then compare them to the professor's answer in the book.

5 WRITE YOUR PARAGRAPH OR ESSAY

In Section 5, students go through the steps of the writing process to a final draft of their unit writing assignment.

STEP 1: BRAINSTORM

Purpose

- To brainstorm, evaluate, and organize ideas for the student paragraph or essay

Teaching Suggestion

After students brainstorm their own ideas on paper, survey the class and list the top three to five ideas for each writing prompt on the board. Then have the students explain, evaluate, and rank the ideas.

STEP 2: MAKE AN OUTLINE

Purpose

- To help students organize their paragraphs or essays before writing

Teaching Suggestion

After students complete their outlines, have them work in pairs to explain how key ideas in their outlines connect to the overall topic or thesis of their paper. This process helps confirm that their ideas are directly relevant to the topic and allows students to consider their ideas more fully.

STEP 3: WRITE YOUR FIRST DRAFT

Purpose

- To give students the opportunity to use the language, skills, and ideas from the unit to answer their writing prompt

Teaching Suggestion

After students write their first drafts, have students work in pairs to give each other feedback before turning in their writing to you. Ask partners to underline sections they think are well-written and circle any words, sentences, or phrases that are unclear. Students can then revise for clarity before submitting their first drafts.

STEP 4: WRITE YOUR FINAL DRAFT

Purpose

- To evaluate and implement instructor/peer feedback
- To improve self-editing skills
- To write a final draft

Teaching Suggestion

Have students mark – highlight, underline, circle, number, etc. – sentences or parts of their writing that they revised based on peer or instructor feedback. This ensures students will incorporate some corrective feedback.

Assessment Program

The final section of the Teacher's Manual consists of an assessment program for *Final Draft*. It includes the following for each unit:

- Vocabulary quiz
- Grammar quiz
- Avoiding Plagiarism quiz
- Bank of additional writing prompts

Quizzes may be used individually or in combination with one or more of the others, depending on teacher and student needs. They are photocopiable, with downloadable versions available at cambridge.org/finaldraft. The Assessment Answer Key includes:

- General rubrics for academic writing (paragraphs / essays)
- Unit answer keys for vocabulary, grammar, and avoiding plagiarism quizzes

1 PARAGRAPHS

EDUCATION: BRAINPOWER

page 13

1 *Answers will vary.*
2 Examples of some things that are easy to remember might include: birthdays or personal information about good friends and family members; information that they use daily, such as addresses or email passwords; or material that they learned in a creative way like associating new vocabulary words with pictures.

1 PREPARE YOUR IDEAS

B Reflect on the Topic page 14

 1.1 page 14

Possible answers: use an app on my phone to remind me; tell someone to remind me; practice the skill or use the information.

2 EXPAND YOUR KNOWLEDGE

A Academic Vocabulary page 16

 2.1 page 16

1 b	3 a	5 a	7 b
2 a	4 a	6 b	8 b

B Academic Collocations page 17

 2.2 page 17

1 c   2 d   3 e   4 b   5 a

C Writing in the Real World page 18

 2.3 page 19

1 *Answers will vary.*
2 c
3 The author recommends hanging out with friends as an excellent brain exercise. Also, interacting at work or at a party is good exercise for the brain.
Possible ideas of other social activities include playing team sports, volunteering at an organization, or participating in a club.

 2.4 page 19

1 This means interacting at work or at a party is good for the brain. Even hanging out with friends is an excellent brain exercise.
2 The first sentence: Finally, brain research suggests that people should never stop learning because learning is brain exercise, too.

3 STUDY ACADEMIC WRITING

A Student Model page 20

Possible answers:

1 The paragraph will be about three things people do to help them remember something.
2 Examples of techniques might include repeating information, writing a note, or setting a reminder on a phone.
3 *Answers will vary.*

Analyze Writing Skills page 20

1 Underlined: People often use three techniques to help them learn new information quickly and easily.
2 Underlined: The second technique is repetition.
Circled: People say or write something again and again.
Double underlined: Many online shoppers are able to remember their credit card number without looking at their card.
3 Circled: For instance
4 Circled: In sum

 3.1 page 21

1 The writer discusses mnemonic devices, repetition, and chunking.
2 b
3 Students' opinions may vary, but chunking works well to memorize a long series of numbers. However, if you used the student ID number many times a day, you would begin to remember it through repetition.

 3.2 pages 21–22

First sentence: People use three techniques to help them learn new information quickly and easily.
Technique 1: A. Mnemonic devices
    Explanation: 1. Short words, music, or rhymes
    Example: 2. FANBOYS

Technique 2: B. Repetition
   Explanation: 1. <u>Say or write something again and again</u>
   Example: 2. <u>Credit card number</u>
Technique 3: C. <u>Chunking</u>
   Explanation: 1. Break something into shorter parts
   Example: 2. Spelling of difficult words, like Wednesday
   Example: 3. <u>Phone numbers</u>
Last sentence: In sum, mnemonic devices, repetition, and chunking are useful techniques that people can use to increase their ability to remember information.

B Paragraphs page 22

 3.3 page 23

1 similar
2 always
3 the same as

 3.4 page 23

1 SS + D
2 CS
3 TS
4 SS + D
5 SS + D

Correct order for paragraph:

   Laughter is good for us because it helps us relax, improves our mood, and strengthens our relationships. First, when we laugh, our muscles relax. We feel less stress. This is good for our hearts. The second reason is that laughter makes us feel better. When we laugh, we feel less sad. We forget our problems for a while. Finally, laughter makes our relationships stronger. People who laugh together feel more connected to each other. In conclusion, laughter has important benefits for our bodies, our minds, and our relationships.

 3.5 page 23

1 (My brain) helps me memorize facts, take interesting photos, and make important decisions.
2 (Eating well) can improve a student's attention span.
3 (Laughter) has many health benefits.
4 (Good soccer players) use their brain in three essential ways.

 3.6 page 24

Possible answers:
2 Eating well <u>can decrease the risks of some diseases.</u>
3 Eating well <u>can improve a student's attention span.</u>
4 Eating well <u>is the best way to avoid weight gain.</u>

 3.7 pages 25–26

1 a too general
  b best: Studying can be more effective if students think creatively.
  c too specific
2 a too specific
  b too general
  c best: There are several ways that people with short attention span can improve their attention span.

 3.8 page 26

Possible answers:
1 Children need loving care, interaction, and healthy food for healthy brain development.
2 My brain helps me be a successful businessperson in three important ways.

 3.10 page 27

   Starting a new job is a stressful experience that makes the brain work its hardest. First, there are many things to learn about the job. <u>When I started my first full-time job, I had to have four hours of training. I took notes, but the manager spoke very fast and explained things very quickly. My brain had to work hard, but I finally learned.</u> Also, there were so many new names to remember. <u>I used fun techniques like matching a word with the person's name. For example, I memorized Harry's name because he always wore a hat.</u> In sum, with a new job there is a lot to remember, but the brain can do it.

3.11 page 28

Possible answers:

1 Students may not know anyone at the school. New students have to learn their way around the school.
2 The brain has to memorize a lot of new things. The brain has to recognize to a lot of new sounds.

3.12 page 28

Possible answers:

Starting a new school is a stressful experience for many students.

The students may not know anyone at the school. This can make them feel isolated and alone.

New students have to learn their way around the school. They can get lost in the new place and frustrated and uncomfortable.

3.14 page 29

1 b   2 a   3 a

3.15 page 30

Possible answers:

1 In sum, my dance teacher taught me that by practicing my steps, watching other dancers, and listening to the music I would learn how to dance.
2 In short, teenagers often act poorly because their brains have not finished developing.

4 SHARPEN YOUR SKILLS

A Writing Skill 1: Audience page 31

4.1 pages 31–32

Students can change unhelpful study habits. One unhealthy habit is that many students stay awake all night to study before a test. This means that they are tired on test day and usually ~~can't~~ *cannot* pay attention. They can change this habit by studying the week before the test. Then they can get enough sleep the night before the test ~~b/c~~ *because*

they are already prepared. Next, it is common for students to procrastinate. They wait until the last minute to do homework and writing assignments. As a result, they ~~don't~~ *do not* have time to ask the teacher questions or do research. ~~You~~ *They* need to start assignments early. Finally, many students ~~wanna~~ *want to* study at home, but there are too many distractions there. For example, they may fall asleep, watch TV, or check Facebook. They could go to the library to study in a quiet place. In short, if ~~you~~ *students* have any of these unhelpful habits, they can change by planning a better study schedule, not procrastinating, and finding a less distracting place to study.

B Writing Skill 2: Capitalization and Punctuation page 32

4.2 page 32

3 correct
4 Some researchers in the United States are creating a map of the brain.
5 Many doctors recommend eating a small meal before studying.

4.3 page 33

People need to practice healthy habits for better mental health. First, a good night's sleep is critical to brain health. Adults need seven to eight hours of sleep each night. When people do not sleep well, they cannot concentrate or remember things well. Also, people need to eat well. Unhealthy foods do not provide the brain with enough energy to work efficiently. Finally, people need to exercise to keep their brains sharp. The brain needs a lot of oxygen to stay healthy, and exercise brings oxygen to the brain. In sum, good sleep, healthy eating, and regular exercise can keep the brain healthy.

C Writing Skill 3: Titles page 34

 4.4 pages 34–35

1 (✓) Title A
Title B: too specific; complete sentence
Title C: too specific
2 Title A: complete sentence
Title B: too general
(✓) Title C
3 Title A: too general
(✓) Title B
Title C: too specific; complete sentence

 4.5 page 35

1 How Positive Thinking Helps the Brain
2 Linking Smell and Memory
3 Mastering a Language
4 Teaching Others Improves Memory

D Grammar for Writing: Adverb Clauses page 35

4.6 page 36

A
1 because
2 while
3 Even though
4 Because
5 even though

B
1 Some people meditate every morning because they say it helps them focus during the day.
2 Exercise helps the brain, while being inactive hurts the brain.
3 Even though students know that they should get more rest before a test, they do not get it.
4 Because jokes exercise our brain, listening to jokes is good for us.
5 My mother prepares healthy foods for our family, even though these foods are often more expensive.

 4.7 page 37

Possible answers:
2 Although my parents do not believe it, listening to music as I write helps me focus.
3 Since all social connections are good for the brain, relationships with family and friends are important for mental health.
4 Because sleep helps people to function well, people should try to get enough sleep.

Avoiding Common Mistakes page 37

 4.8 page 38

Although cooking does not seem like an intellectual activity to some, ~~but~~ it can provide some benefits to the brain. First of all, it can be a way for people to learn new skills. If people try making new recipes from different cultures, for example, the brain has to learn skills and ideas. Learning is good for the brain. ~~Because~~ *because* it makes the brain work hard. Also, cooking can be a physical activity. Although cooking is not as physical as jogging or playing soccer, ~~but~~ it still requires effort. This effort brings oxygen to the brain. The brain needs oxygen to work well. Finally, cooking can provide social interaction. ~~Althought~~ *Although* cooking does not have to be social, it can be. People join cooking classes or cook with friends at home. Social activities like these are beneficial for the brain. ~~Because~~ *because* building relationships makes people feel closer and less stressed. This is good for the brain. In short, cooking is a necessity, but it can also help the brain function better.

E Avoiding Plagiarism page 39

 4.9 page 40

Student C:
Several studies show that exercise is good for the brain. For example, older people <u>who take regular walks can pay attention better</u>. Also, <u>jogging regularly improves memory</u>. Exercise is even good for mice. When they ran, <u>they could learn and remember better than other mice</u>.

Student D:
Exercise leads to good brain health. <u>Exercise improves brain function in older people. People who go for regular walks pay attention better.</u> Jogging is also a good exercise. It leads to better memory. In other research, <u>when mice ran on a small wheel, they got more blood into their brains.</u> This led to better learning and remembering for the mice.

 **ESSENTIAL FEATURES OF EFFECTIVE WRITING**

COMMUNICATIONS: CROSS-CULTURAL BEHAVIOR

page 45

Possible answers:

1 My teacher or foreign friend and I can have different feelings about the same city, movie, or news event.
2 In my culture it is polite to take off your shoes in someone else's house. It is impolite to be late for an appointment.
3 Yes, before I had children, I thought parents with noisy, crazy children were lazy parents. After I had children, I changed my mind.

1 PREPARE YOUR IDEAS

Ⓑ Reflect on the Topic page 46

 1.1 page 46

Topic: Sports fans at a sporting event
Additional ideas: carrying noisemakers, wearing team caps, sitting in the area of other team supporters.

2 EXPAND YOUR KNOWLEDGE

Ⓐ Academic Vocabulary page 48

2.1 page 48

1 a	3 b	5 a	7 a
2 b	4 a	6 b	8 b

Ⓑ Academic Phrases page 49

2.2 page 49

1 c   2 a   3 b

Ⓒ Writing in the Real World page 50

2.3 page 51

1 the OK sign, thumbs-up, eye contact, touching
2 *Answers will vary.*
3 *Answers will vary.*

2.4 page 51

1 four
2 The different types are described in separate paragraphs: OK sign, thumbs up, eye contact, greeting customs
Paragraphs put similar ideas together and clearly show when a topic changes.

3 STUDY ACADEMIC WRITING

Ⓐ Student Model page 52
Possible answers:
1 The paragraph will be about the etiquette of behavior in large gatherings.
2 The writer could include behaviors such as dressing up in costumes, dancing, shouting, jumping, and singing.

Analyze Writing Skills page 52
1 Underlined: In many cultures, people's behavior at sports events is very different from their everyday behavior.
Circled: behavior at sports events
2 3 supporting ideas
3 Circled: Furthermore, Lastly
4 Yes
5 Underlined: In short, people at sports events show unusual behavior that is different from their behavior in their everyday lives.

3.1 page 53

1 clothing, yelling, and physical contact
2 *Answers will vary.*
3 *Answers will vary.*

3.2 page 53

Topic sentence: In many cultures, people's behavior at sports events is very different from their everyday behavior.
Behavior 1: A. Wearing team colors
 Detail: 1. <u>Hats, shirts, jackets</u>
 Detail: 2. Bright colors
Behavior 2: B. <u>Yelling and screaming</u>
 Detail: 1. Encouragement to own team
 Detail: 2. <u>Insulting the opposite team</u>
Behavior 3: C. Physical contact with strangers
 Detail: 1. High-fives
 Detail: 2. <u>Hugging</u>
Concluding sentence: In short, people at sporting events show unusual behavior that is different from their behavior in their everyday lives.

B Coherence page 54

 3.3 page 55

1 spatial
 Underline: in the front, in the back, in the middle
2 rank
 Underline: One method, Another very useful method, Finally
3 chronological
 Underline: First, After that, Finally

 3.4 page 56

Possible answers:
1 chronological or rank
2 chronological
3 spatial or rank

 3.6 page 57

1 First,
2 Furthermore,
3 For example,
4 In addition,
5 In conclusion,

 3.7 page 57

Possible answers:
2 After that, their friend will often call out, "Come in!"
3 In addition, some people may send a small gift.

4 On the other hand, in some professions men wear suits and ties.
5 For instance, nodding or bowing to greet someone is polite in some countries.
6 Then they will take their guests' coats and offer them beverages.

4 SHARPEN YOUR SKILLS

A Writing Skill 1: Unity page 58

 4.1 page 59

Cross out:
A child's first birthday is one year after the birth.
I have never been to a baby shower, but I would like to go to one.

B Writing Skill 2: Subject–Verb Agreement page 59

 4.2 page 60

Active Listeners Make Good Listeners

1 is	5 do not	9 say	13 help
2 shows	6 shows	10 know	14 is
3 is	7 is	11 are	
4 talks	8 gives	12 ask	

C Grammar for Writing: Quantifiers page 60

 4.3 page 61

Possible answers:
1 ~~Women~~ *Some women* talk more than men do.
2 ~~Teenagers~~ *A number of teenagers* do not know social rules.
3 ~~Teenagers~~ *Few teenagers* know the etiquette for social situations.
4 ~~Children~~ *Quite a few children* do not stay quiet while adults are talking.
5 ~~Children~~ *Many children* kiss their older relatives to say hello.

Avoiding Common Mistakes page 62

 4.4 page 62

                number

A large ~~amount~~ of people around the world are using social media sites like Facebook, Twitter, and Instagram, but few ~~of~~ users know the basic etiquette. The first rule is to avoid sharing all of your thoughts. A few ~~of~~ friends probably share every piece of information from their day, but not everyone wants to hear what they had for lunch. Another rule is to think carefully before adding photos that include other people. Sharing some photos may be embarrassing to others, so it is polite to ask your friends for permission. For example, ask friends before adding any photos of them in

            A number

swimsuits. ~~An amount~~ of fights between friends happen when they make negative comments on each other's web page. Making positive comments

               a

will help avoid problems and show ^ little respect.

     a number

Finally, ~~an amount~~ of businesses are now searching social media sites before they hire new employees. If they see crazy pictures or a lot of complaints on a person's website, they will not hire that person. In conclusion, it is important to think carefully before sharing any information on the Internet.

Ⓓ Avoiding Plagiarism page 63

 4.5 page 63

Possible answers:
Strategy 1: She shouldn't listen to anyone who suggests that she copy from the Internet. It's against the school's academic integrity policy.
Strategy 2: She should ask her teacher for help.

❸ DESCRIPTIVE PARAGRAPHS

GLOBAL STUDIES: NATIONAL IDENTITIES

page 67

1 *Possible answer:* National identity is how people think about a nation or country and the qualities of a nation that make it different from other nations.
2 *Answers will vary.*
3 *Possible answer:* National identity may come from a shared history, language, religion, or challenges.

1 PREPARE YOUR IDEAS

Answers will vary.

2 EXPAND YOUR KNOWLEDGE

Ⓐ Academic Vocabulary page 70

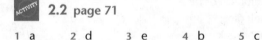 **2.1** pages 70–71

A
1 c	2 d	3 a	4 b

B
1 a	2 d	3 c	4 b

Ⓑ Academic Collocations page 71

2.2 page 71

1 a	2 d	3 e	4 b	5 c

Ⓒ Writing in the Real World page 72

 2.3 page 73

1 the melting pot, a salad, chocolate fondue. The author believes the last one is the most accurate because people can be part of the U.S. and still keep their own identity.
2 Making English the official language of the United States supports the idea of assimilation because it asks everyone to speak the same language.
3 *Answers will vary.*

Possible answers:

1 a small porcelain bowl on a table in a laboratory
  the flame grows taller and taller
  it turns different colors – orange, red, blue, white
2 leafy, green lettuce
  round, red tomatoes
  skinny, orange carrots

3 STUDY ACADEMIC WRITING

Student Model page 74

Possible answers:

1 The paragraph will be about an important celebration in one country. It will give descriptions of the celebration and show why it is important to the people and their ethnic or national identity.
2 food, special clothing and music, special performances, parades, ways of celebrating, the reason for the celebration

Analyze Writing Skills pages 74–75

1 Underlined: *El Grito de Dolores* is an important national celebration in Mexico and an important part of Mexico's national identity.
  Circled: *El Grito de Dolores*
2 Underlined: hang the Mexican flag from their houses and cars; lights, balloons, and pinwheels in the streets and on the buildings; everything is red, white and green
3 Circled: excited
4 Yes

1 decorations, people gathering, reenactment of *El Grito*
2 Mexican flags on houses and cars; lights, balloons, and pinwheels in the streets and on the buildings; red, white, and green decorations
3 *Possible answer:* They feel proud of him and thankful because he started the war for independence.

Topic Sentence: *El Grito de Dolores* is an important national celebration in Mexico and an important part of Mexico's national identity.
  Feature 1: A. The decorations
    Detail 1. Flags
    Detail 2. Lights, balloons, and pinwheels
    Detail 3. Red, white, and green colors
  Feature 2: B. The gathering
    Detail 1. Traditional clothing, music, and food
    Detail 2. Locations: in town centers, at el Zócalo, on TV
    Detail 3. Crowded and excited
  Feature 3: C. The reenactment
    Detail 1. Important history
    Detail 2. Leader rings a bell and cries
    Detail 3. Fireworks, national anthem, "Viva Mexico"!

Concluding sentence: *El Grito de Dolores* is a special and important celebration for the people of Mexico.

Descriptive Paragraphs page 77

1 golden torch, seven-point crown, broken chains
2 The writer chose the features because they are symbols of freedom that the writer wants the reader to understand.
3 **The torch: sensory details** – light in the darkness
  The crown: spatial location – on her head
  The crown: facts and relevant information – means the light of freedom
  The chains: spatial location – at the bottom of the statue; around her feet
  The chains: feelings – free

1 On the left
2 At the bottom
3 in the center
4 On the right
5 in front

3.7 page 81

Underlined sensory details:

An important part of any national identity is the food or drinks that are traditional in the country, such as çay in Turkey. Çay, or Turkish tea, is central to Turkish hospitality. The most popular çay is a <u>special black tea</u> from the coast of the Black Sea. It has a <u>strong taste</u>, and some say it has a <u>slight orange flavor</u>. Çay is traditionally served in a small <u>tulip-shaped clear glass</u>. This allows people to see its <u>dark brown color</u>. Many tea drinkers add water to make the tea <u>lighter</u> in color and <u>less strong</u> in taste. The glass does not have handles. Therefore, servers cannot fill it to the top. People need a place to hold the cup without <u>burning their fingers on the hot glass</u>. The tea is always served with one or two <u>white sugar cubes</u>. Many add this sugar to make the tea <u>very sweet</u>. It is common for Turkish people to gather together in cafés to drink çay with friends and family, and this tea is almost always served to guests in Turkish homes.

Words and phrases in chart:

Sight: special black (tea); small tulip-shaped clear (glass); dark brown (color); one or two white (sugar cubes); lighter

Sound: N/A

Smell: N/A

Taste: strong (taste); slight orange (flavor); less strong; very sweet

Touch: burning their fingers on the hot glass

 3.11 page 84

1 c   2 b   3 a

4 SHARPEN YOUR SKILLS

 Writing Skill 1: Vivid Language
   page 85

 4.1 page 85

Possible answers:

1 gigantic   4 exciting
2 bright   5 joyful
3 noisy

 Writing Skill 2: Avoiding Sentence Fragments, Run-ons, and Comma Splices page 86

 4.2 page 87

1 C   2 R   3 F   4 C   5 F

 4.3 page 87

Possible answers:

1 Americans celebrate their struggle for independence on the Fourth of July. This day is a national holiday.

2 A country's money often has interesting images and designs. They reveal important social values or history.

3 New York City is a diverse city. For example, it has neighborhoods with many different ethnic restaurants and stores.

4 Ecuador has amazing natural resources. Many Ecuadorians are concerned about protecting their wild animals, plants, and lands.

5 There are many Canadian families with a Chinese ethnic background. Therefore, many Canadians celebrate Chinese holidays, like Chinese New Year.

 Writing Skill 3: Correct Pronoun Use page 87

 4.4 page 88

1 They   5 it
2 He   6 his
3 They   7 their
4 him   8 themselves

 Grammar for Writing: Adjectives page 89

 4.5 page 90

1 excited   4 surprised
2 amazing   5 disappointed
3 interesting

 4.6 page 90

1 American   4 Canadian
2 Spanish   5 Korean
3 Jamaican

Avoiding Common Mistakes page 91

 4.7 page 91

Soccer is not just a sport in Brazil. Some

~~brazilians~~ ^{Brazilians} consider soccer to be like a religion.

Most agree that soccer is a national passion.

Like many nations, the people of ~~brazil~~ ^{Brazil} are very

diverse. There are many different social classes and

ethnic groups. However, almost everyone in Brazil

is ~~interest~~ ^{interested} in the Brazilian national soccer team.

When the national team is playing, most Brazilian

citizens are ~~worry~~ ^{worried}. Will they win or will they lose?

Brazilians are united in their concern for their

country's team. Thousands of ~~brazilian~~ ^{Brazilian} fans go

to the soccer games. The fans are ~~exciting~~ ^{excited}. They

cheer or sing loudly in ~~portugese~~ ^{Portuguese}. They wear their

team's colors: blue, green, and yellow. They wave

huge Brazilian flags. These soccer games bring the

people together to cheer for their team. Soccer is

an important part of Brazil's national identity.

 4.8 page 93

1 CK	3 NCK	5 CK	7 CK
2 CK	4 NCK	6 NCK	

④ DEFINITION PARAGRAPHS

BUSINESS: WORKPLACE BEHAVIOR

page 97

Possible answers:

1 Doctors with dead plants seem like they cannot take good care of living things, including patients.

2 Good doctors listen to their patients and take their time. Bad doctors are very quick and uncaring.

3 Never go to an automobile mechanic who doesn't drive. Never go to a doctor who smokes.

1 PREPARE YOUR IDEAS

Answers will vary.

2 EXPAND YOUR KNOWLEDGE

Ⓐ Academic Vocabulary page 100

 2.1 page 100

1 b	3 a	5 b	7 a
2 b	4 a	6 a	8 b

Ⓑ Academic Phrases page 101

 2.2 page 101

1 c	2 a	3 b

Ⓒ Writing in the Real World page 102

 2.3 page 103

1 shared work space, cell phones, social media

2 *Answers will vary.*

3 *Possible answer:* Problems with technology. Sometimes people can't complete their work because their computers don't work.

 2.4 page 103

1 The author defines *open work spaces*. Some details include: a definition (areas with no walls; co-workers sit next to each other); purpose (encourages working together); problems (noise, conflicts between co-workers, no behavior policies).

2 She gives examples of social media: websites like Facebook or Twitter. She talks about posting personal photos and information.

3 STUDY ACADEMIC WRITING

Ⓐ Student Model page 104

1 a team player

2 *Answers will vary.*

Analyze Writing Skills page 104

1 Underlined: The *Cambridge Learner's Dictionary* definition of *team player* is "member of a group who tries to do what is good for the group rather than what is good for just himself or herself."
Circled: team player

2 b

3 Underlined: he does not try to make people feel bad

4 a coach

5 Underlined: For instance, waiters who are team players help clean off each other's tables when the restaurant gets busy.

 3.1 page 105

1 *Possible answers:* He is a good speaker and listener. He is always polite. He is like a coach. He encourages others to share. He helps his co-workers. He does any job.

2 *Answers will vary.*

3 *Answers will vary.*

 3.2 page 106

Topic Sentence: The *Cambridge Learner's Dictionary* definition of *team player* is "member of a group who tries to do what is good for the group rather than what is good for just himself or herself."

Supporting Sentence 1: A. <u>Co-worker who communicates clearly</u>

  Detail: 1. Good speaker and listener
  Detail: 2. <u>Shares opinions</u>
  Detail: 3. Avoids conflict
  Detail: 4. Requests politely

Supporting Sentence 2: B. Supports co-workers

  Detail: 1. Helps co-workers
  Detail: 2. Behaves respectfully
  Detail: 3. <u>Like a coach; gives encouragement</u>

Supporting Sentence 3: C. <u>Does any job</u>

  Detail: 1. Does not say "not my job"
  Detail: 2. <u>Waiters who clean each other's tables</u>

Concluding Sentence: In brief, a team player is a valuable player on any workplace team.

B Definition Paragraphs page 107

 3.3 page 107

The writer is defining the term differently than the definition. He is defining it for the workplace: *However, it has a different meaning in the workplace.*

 3.4 page 108

1 An (intern) is a <u>person</u> <u>who is learning about a job while doing it</u>.

2 A (cubicle) is a <u>work space</u> <u>with low walls around it</u>.

3 (Conflict resolution) is <u>the process of</u> <u>solving problems between two people or two groups</u>.

4 A (rookie) is a <u>person</u> <u>who has just started a new job or activity</u>.

5 (Respect) is a <u>feeling</u> <u>that you have when you admire someone for their qualities or abilities</u>.

 3.5 page 108

A

Possible answers:

1 A work space is an area that has everything a worker needs to complete his or her work.

2 A cashier is a person who adds up your purchases and takes your money.

3 A hairdresser is a person who styles your hair.

4 Salary is the money that you get for doing your job.

B

Answers will vary.

 3.7 page 109

Possible answers:

1 C   2 SE   3 I, SE   4 NE   5 I, SE

 3.8 page 110

Possible answers:

1 A co-worker is like a classmate but is at your job.

2 Vacation time is not sick time because you can choose to use it for fun.

3 For example, a co-worker helps another co-worker do research for a report.

4 Punctuality in the Philippines means being less than 30 minutes late.

4 SHARPEN YOUR SKILLS

A Writing Skill 1: Distinguishing Between Fact and Opinion page 111

 4.1 page 112

1 O   2 O   3 F   4 O   5 F   6 O

B Writing Skill 2: Verb Tense Consistency

4.3 page 114

According to the *Cambridge Learner's Dictionary* online, a wallet <u>is</u> a "small, folding case for paper money and credit cards." In other words, it <u>is</u> a way to carry money. A wallet ~~was~~ [is] similar to a bank because both <u>hold</u> money. Also, people <u>put</u> money into both a bank and a wallet. In addition, people ~~took~~ [take] money out of both a bank and a wallet. However, a wallet <u>is</u> different from a bank in some ways. A bank <u>is</u> a safe way to keep money, and it <u>can</u> hold a great deal of money. A wallet <u>is</u> not a safe way to keep money. Wallets ~~were~~ [are] not very big, so they <u>cannot</u> hold a lot of money. For example, my wallet <u>does not have</u> very much money right now. A year ago, it ~~has~~ [had] a lot of money because I ~~have~~ [had] a good job at that time. I ~~don't have~~ [didn't have] enough money to fill a bank then, but I <u>had</u> enough money to fill my wallet. Someday, I ~~had~~ [have] a good job again, and my wallet <u>will be</u> full of money again.

4.4 page 114

2 pays	6 is	10 say
3 allows	7 exceeds	11 hurts
4 is	8 make	12 believe
5 has	9 is	13 will help

C Writing Skill 3: Coordinating Conjunctions

4.6 page 116

Possible answers:

1 or	4 and
2 , but	5 , but
3 , so	6 and

4.7 page 116

Possible answers:

1 Many companies are trying to protect the environment, <u>so they are creating a "green workplace."</u>
2 Recycling takes a lot of time and energy<u>, but it is worth it.</u>
3 Working in an office all day long is tiring<u>, so it is important to take frequent work breaks.</u>
4 Doing a good job is very satisfying <u>and profitable.</u>
5 It is important to distinguish between <u>fact and opinion.</u>
6 Some people like Google's pet policy<u>, so they bring their pets to work.</u>

D Grammar for Writing page 117

4.8 page 117

2 These <u>meals</u> [CP] can happen at the <u>workplace</u> [CS] or another <u>location</u> [CS].
3 The <u>conversation</u> [CP] may include <u>small talk</u> [NC] about <u>topics</u> [CP] such as the current <u>news</u> [NC], <u>sports</u> [CP], or <u>movies</u> [CP].
4 The <u>behavior</u> [NC] is more casual at these <u>lunches</u> [CP].
5 <u>Employees</u> [CP] often dislike work <u>lunches</u> [CP] because they do not get a <u>break</u> [CS] from <u>work</u> [NC].

Avoiding Common Mistakes page 118

4.9 page 118

Job success is achieving goals and feeling satisfied with your work. Many people believe that a success is making a lot of ~~moneys~~ [money], but money does not bring ~~many~~ [much] satisfaction to everybody. However, workers can feel success and ~~a~~ [a] satisfaction from setting goal and reaching that goal. In addition, if [an] **employee** is happy with his or her duties, he or she is more likely to do well. Enjoyable work and meeting goals are very important for ~~successes~~ [success].

E Avoiding Plagiarism page 119

 4.10 page 120

Check: 1, 2

 4.11 page 120

1 b   2 a   3 b

5 INTRODUCTION TO THE ESSAY: OPINION ESSAYS

PSYCHOLOGY: CREATIVITY

page 125

Possible answers:

1 Creativity is using your imagination to make new things.
2 I agree. For example, artists who make a lot of art and writers who write a lot often get better and become more creative.
3 artists, designers, chefs, architects

1 PREPARE YOUR IDEAS

Answers will vary.

2 EXPAND YOUR KNOWLEDGE

A Academic Vocabulary page 128

 2.1 pages 128–129

1 a	3 b	5 b	7 b
2 b	4 a	6 a	8 b

B Academic Collocations page 129

 2.2 page 129

1 d   2 c   3 b   4 e   5 a

C Writing in the Real World page 130

 2.3 page 131

1 The main reasons why the author thinks high schools should require classes in the arts are that the arts help students in other subjects and keep students from dropping out of school.

2 The author supports her opinion with a story about a former student who benefitted from arts classes, as well as statistics from research studies on the effects of arts classes on test scores, IQ tests, memory, motivation, and attendance.

3 *Answers will vary.*

 2.4 page 131

1 The author tries to make the readers interested in the topic in paragraphs 1 and 2. She gives her opinion in paragraph 4.
2 The author gives two main reasons, which are found in paragraphs 5 and 6.
3 In the first sentence of the last paragraph.

3 STUDY ACADEMIC WRITING

A Student Model page 132

Possible answers:

1 The arts show history and culture. This is important to know because it can help all subjects. The arts are part of what makes a person an educated individual. The arts are more relaxing than other "academic" subjects.

2 The arts are a waste of time because you can never use them in everyday life. The arts are uninteresting and therefore studying about them will be unnecessarily difficult. There is no time to study the arts with all the other required subjects.

3 *Answers will vary.*

Analyze Writing Skills pages 132–133

1 Underlined: High schools should not make students take classes in the arts for three main reasons: these classes do not prepare students for college, they are too expensive, and students do not have time for them.

2 Underlined: Paragraph 2: The first reason why classes in the arts should not be required is that these classes do not prepare students for college.

Paragraph 3: Another reason for my opinion is that classes in the arts cost too much money. These classes need a wide range of expensive equipment such as paint, musical instruments, or video cameras.

Paragraph 4: The final reason that high school students should not have to take classes in the arts is that they do not have enough time to explore these subjects.

The topics are **the same as** the topics in the last sentence in paragraph 1.

3 Circled: in conclusion
4 a recommendation

3.1 page 134

1 No, she doesn't.
2 She thinks that classes in the arts do not prepare students for college, are too expensive, and students do not have time for them.
3 *Answers will vary.*

 3.2 page 134

I Introductory Paragraph
Thesis Statement: High schools should not make students take classes in the art for three main reasons: these classes do not prepare students for college, they are too expensive, and students do not have time for them.
Body Paragraph 1, Reason 1:
II Doesn't prepare students for college
  Supporting Sentence: A. What college applications require
    Detail: 1. Grades
    Detail: 2. Test scores
    Detail: 3. Essay
  Supporting Sentence: B. Arts not required on applications
  Supporting Sentence: C. Most students not art majors
Body Paragraph 2, Reason 2:
III Classes too expensive
  Supporting Sentence: A. Equipment is expensive
    Detail: 1. Paint
    Detail: 2. Musical instruments
    Detail: 3. Video cameras
  Supporting Sentence: B. Other subjects more important
    Detail: 1. Chemistry
    Detail: 2. Biology
  Supporting Sentence: C. Students can't afford equipment
Body Paragraph 3, Reason 3:
IV No time for arts classes
  Supporting Sentence: A. Students already busy
    Detail: 1. Classes
    Detail: 2. Homework
    Detail: 3. Preparing for college entrance tests
  Supporting Sentence: B. No time for the arts
V Concluding Paragraph
Concluding Sentence: Instead of spending money on the arts, high schools should offer more tutoring and test preparation.

 B From Paragraph to Essay page 136

 3.3 page 137

1 similar to
2 topic sentence
3 usually restates

 3.4 page 137

1 b   2 a   3 a   4 a   5 b

C Opinion Essays page 138

3.5 page 139

A

  Throughout history, there have always been artists and other creative people, and they have often struggled to earn a living. One example of this is the famous painter Vincent van Gogh. He only sold one painting during his life and was often poor and hungry. Today, we all enjoy van Gogh's work, and he might have made even more wonderful paintings if he had received more support. Luckily, today there are many programs that give money to help artists, including some government programs. In my view, the city government ought to do more to support artists because this will create more art for everyone to enjoy, it will attract tourists, and it will encourage more young people to be artists.

B

1 It will be about whether governments should do more to support artists.
2 It is to give background information about the topic.
3 The writer's opinion is that governments should do more to support the arts.
4 Three reasons: Government support will create more art for everyone to enjoy, attract tourists, and encourage more people to be artists.

 3.6 page 140

1 b   2 a   3 a   4 b

3.7 page 140

Possible answers:

Check: 2, 3, 5

1 The statement doesn't answer the question. The question is whether parents should encourage children to become artists, but the statement is about why artists don't earn enough money.

4 The statement doesn't give one clear opinion. It gives two conflicting opinions: children should be encouraged, but sometimes it is better not to be an artist.

 3.9 page 142

1 Circled: Body paragraph 1: The first reason why modern and contemporary art should not be worth very high prices is that anyone can make it.

Body paragraph 2: Another reason for my opinion is that today's art is often made from materials that have no value.

2 Body paragraph 1 reason: Anyone can make contemporary art, so it isn't valuable.

Body paragraph 2 reason: Contemporary art is made from cheap materials, so it isn't worth a lot of money.

3 Underlined: Body paragraph 1: Today's art can be made with very little skill or talent.

Body paragraph 2: Some artists work with very cheap materials.

4 Dotted line: Body paragraph 1:

For example, paintings by the artist Jackson Pollock have sold for over $100 million … (example)

He just dripped, poured, and squirted … (fact)

Anyone can do that. (explanation)

One example of this is the French artist Marcel Duchamp. (example)

In 1917, Duchamp bought a toilet at a hardware store and … (fact)

The critics said he was a genius, (fact)

but anyone could do that. (explanation)

More recently, the British artist Tracey Emin … (example)

Someone paid £150,000 for it. (fact)

This price is not reasonable because nearly all of us already have a bed and do not need to buy one … (explanation)

Body paragraph 2:

The American artist Tom Friedman is an example of this. (example)

He has made expensive art from toothpicks, pieces of tape … (fact)

Recently, Friedman put a single green pea … (fact / example)

This is not a reasonable price. No one will want to eat a pea … (explanation)

There are even artists, such as the American artist Joseph Cornell … (example)

Today, people pay more than $100,000 … (fact)

5 Circled: Anyone could make it; it is often made from worthless things.

The reasons are the same.

 3.10 pages 142–143

Possible answers:

Body paragraph 1. One reason why we need more programs about the arts is <u>these programs are educational</u>.

Body paragraph 2. Another reason for my opinion is that <u>they make viewers more creative</u>.

Body paragraph 3. Finally, television channels ought to have more programs about the arts because <u>these programs help support artists</u>.

 3.11 page 143

Possible answers:

Reason 1: relaxing

Reason 2: keep your mind sharp

Reason 3: you might discover you have a lot of talent

 3.12 page 143

Possible answers:

Topic sentence 1. The first reason for my opinion that everyone should have a creative hobby is that hobbies are relaxing.

Topic sentence 2. Another reason for my opinion is that creative hobbies keep your mind sharp.

Topic sentence 3. Finally, it is a good idea to have a creative hobby because you might discover you have a lot of talent.

 3.13 page 144

Possible answers:

Body paragraph 1

Supporting sentence: Creative hobbies help you forget your problems.

Detail: If you are focused on a painting, you will not think about your bad day at work.

Body paragraph 2

Supporting sentence: Some creative hobbies improve your memory.

Detail: Musicians can play very long songs from memory, without using sheet music.

Body paragraph 3

Supporting sentence: Many famous artists only started late in life.

Detail: Grandma Moses, a famous American painter, only started painting when she was quite old.

 3.14 page 144

Possible answers:

The first reason why everyone should have a creative hobby is that hobbies are relaxing. Creative hobbies help you forget your problems. If you are focused on a painting, you will not think about your bad day at work. In addition, creative hobbies reduce your stress. Scientists have learned that people who have creative hobbies have lower blood pressure, which means they are less stressed.

 3.16 page 146

1 Underlined: In my view this is a bad thing because the world needs creative adults to invent new products, to entertain us with books and movies, and to solve important problems in the world.

2 Underlined: Because we need creativity for inventions, entertainment, and solutions to major problems, in my opinion it is a shame that so many adults are not creative.

3 Circled in thesis statement: invent new products, entertain us, solve important problems

Circled in conclusion: inventions, entertainment, solutions to major problems

4 Dotted line: To summarize

5 Boxed: For this reason, all adults should spend at least an hour each day doing something creative, such as writing or painting. (recommendation)

 3.17 pages 146–147

1 c

Reason: a. does not include all of the reasons in the thesis statement; b. adds an extra reason not given in the thesis.

2 b

Reason: a. adds an extra reason not given in the thesis and does not include all of the reasons in the thesis; c. does not include all of the reasons in the thesis.

3 a

Reason: b. does not include all of the reasons in the thesis statement; c. adds a reason not given in the thesis.

 3.18 page 147

b

4 SHARPEN YOUR SKILLS

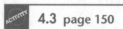

A Writing Skill 1: Background Information page 148

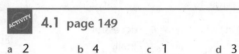 **4.1** page 149

a 2   b 4   c 1   d 3

4.2 page 149

a

4.3 page 150

Possible answer: Many people are very creative when they are children but become less creative when they are adults.

B Writing Skill 2: The Thesis Statement page 150

 **4.5** page 151

A

1 O   2 R   3 T   4 O

B

Possible answers:

2 today's art is not beautiful and the money should go to charity instead

3 people spend millions of dollars on art

4 should not spend millions of dollars on art

4.6 pages 151–152

Possible answers:

1 There should be more arts programming on TV because it educates people, it is relaxing, and it will support artists.

2 In my opinion knowledge is more important than imagination because we need knowledge to make useful things, to do well in school, and to get a good job.

3 In my view, people should not buy expensive art because anyone can make it, because art should be affordable to everyone, and because it should be in public museums.

◉ Grammar for Writing: Word Forms
page 152

 4.8 page 154

1 conclusion
2 creative
3 independence
4 confidence
5 confident
6 successful
7 Finally
8 motivate
9 creativity

Avoiding Common Mistakes page 155

 4.9 page 155

       difference
One ~~differance~~ between children and adults is that adults are often less creative. In my view that is a good thing because we need adults to
       useful
do jobs that are ~~usefull~~ and helpful but are not always creative. For example, we need people to build important things like bridges, and people need to know that these are safe so they can
     confidence   *really*
use them with ~~confidance~~. This work is not ~~realy~~ creative, but it has a lot of importance. If adults were as creative as children, they might not want to do this sort of work. We also need doctors and
               wonderful
nurses to keep us healthy. These are ~~wonderfull~~
                 patience
and important jobs that require a lot of ~~patiance~~, skill, and knowledge. However, they do not require as much creativity as a career in the arts.

       Finally
~~Finaly~~, our country needs police officers and soldiers to protect us. People in these jobs have to follow orders and do not have many chances to be creative. In sum, because there are many important jobs that do not require creativity, it is a good thing that many adults are less creative than children.

◉ Avoiding Plagiarism page 156

 4.10 page 157

The writer used three ways. First, he used an in-text citation. Then he cited the author at the end of the quote. Finally, he put the author's exact words in quotations.

 4.11 page 157

Some argue that older people are not as creative as younger people. <u>According to Moody, it is true that older people take longer to learn new things, and their reactions are slower (359)</u>. However, he believes older people can still be creative. <u>Moody says, "Creativity can mean doing old things in a new way, or in a different way"(qtd. in Collins 3).</u> If people learn new things, they can be creative all of their life (Bahrampour 6).

 **CLASSIFICATION ESSAYS**

HEALTH: FOOD IN SOCIETY

page 163

1 *Possible answer:* If a person is a vegetarian, for example, this might tell us many things. Perhaps the person is vegetarian for religious reasons, for health reasons, because he or she cares about animals, or because he or she is worried about the effect that raising animals for meat has on the environment.

2 *Answers will vary.*

3 *Answers will vary.*

1 PREPARE YOUR IDEAS

Answers will vary.

2 EXPAND YOUR KNOWLEDGE

Academic Vocabulary page 166

 2.1 page 166

1 b   3 b   5 b   7 b
2 a   4 a   6 a   8 a

Academic Phrases page 167

2.2 page 167

1 b   2 c   3 a

C Writing in the Real World page 168

2.3 page 169

Possible answers:

1 The two kinds of food are "hot" foods that warm the body and "cool" foods that cool it. Some examples of hot foods are lamb, peppers, cinnamon, and ginger. Some examples of cool foods are watermelon, corn, pork, and tofu.

2 You should eat hot foods when you are cool, or when you have an illness that is "cool." You should eat cool foods when you are hot or have a "hot" illness.

3 *Answers will vary.*

2.4 page 169

1 All food is divided into two categories: hot and cool.

2 In traditional Chinese medicine, most illnesses can also be classified as hot or cool.

3 STUDY ACADEMIC WRITING

Student Model page 170

Analyze Writing Skills pages 170–171

1 Underlined: at supermarkets, at farmers' markets, and in your own garden.
Three categories are mentioned.

2 Underlined: One place to get fruit and vegetables

3 Checked: cost, convenience, quality

4 Yes

5 In conclusion, farmers' markets, supermarkets, and your own garden are three places to get fruit and vegetables, and all of them have good points and bad points.

 3.1 page 172

1 supermarkets, farmers' markets, and your own garden

2 Supermarkets: cost can be low or high, quality can be good or poor, and supermarkets are convenient because every town has at least one. Growing your own: cost is very low, quality is very good, but it is not convenient because it takes time and work.

Farmers' markets: cost is often less than supermarkets, quality is usually very high, but they are not convenient because most neighborhoods do not have a farmers' market.

3 Farmers' markets are best, if one is nearby, because they are sometimes less expensive and the quality is usually good.

3.2 pages 172–173

1 Introductory Paragraph
Thesis Statement: In the United States, the main places to get fruit and vegetables are at supermarkets, at <u>farmers' markets</u>, and in your own garden, and each place has advantages and disadvantages.

Body Paragraph 1, Category 1:

II Supermarkets

    Detail/characteristic: A. Cost

        Explanation: 1. Cheap in some places

        Explanation: 2. <u>Expensive in others</u>

    Detail/characteristic: B. Quality

        Explanation: 1. Sometimes imported, not fresh, chemicals

        Explanation: 2. <u>Sometimes organic,</u> fresher, more expensive

    Detail/Characteristic: C. Convenience

        Explanation: 1. Usually one in every town

        Explanation: 2. Convenient for most people

Body Paragraph 2, Category 2:

III Farmers' markets

    Detail/characteristic: A. Cost: <u>lower than supermarkets</u>

        Explanation: 1. Local farmers

        Explanation: 2. Local produce

    Detail/characteristic: B. Quality: <u>better than supermarkets</u>

        Explanation: 1. Fresh

        Explanation: 2. No chemicals

    Detail/characteristic: C. Convenience: not for everyone

        Explanation: 1. Sometimes in big cities

        Explanation: 2. Not in most places

Body Paragraph 3, Category 3:

IV Growing your own

    Detail/characteristic: A. Cost: low

        Explanation: 1. Cheap seeds

        Explanation: 2. Needs dirt, water, time

    Detail/characteristic: B. Quality: very good

        Explanation: 1. <u>Not pretty but fresh</u>

        Explanation: 2. Taste better

    Detail/characteristic: C. Convenience: not for everyone

        Explanation: 1. Requires special tools

        Explanation: 2. Takes time and space

V Concluding Paragraph

    Concluding Sentence: The best place to buy produce is probably at farmers' markets, if one is nearby, because the prices are often low and the quality is usually high.

Classification Essays page 174

 3.3 page 175

1 c, e, f

2 a

3 In the United States, the main places to get fruit and vegetables are at supermarkets, at farmers' markets, and in your own garden, and each place has advantages and disadvantages.

4 In conclusion, farmers' markets, supermarkets, and your own garden are three places to get fruit and vegetables, and all of them have good points and bad points.

 3.4 page 176

Check: Student 2

Write X: Students 1, 3, 4

Student 1's categories do not cover the topic completely. There are many food businesses that do not belong to any of these categories, such as restaurants. Also, shopping malls are not mainly food businesses.

Student 3's categories are not different enough from each other. These are all kinds of supermarkets, and many businesses would belong to more than one category.

Student 4's categories are not related to the topic of the writing prompt. The topic is businesses based on food, but these categories seem to be kinds of people who do not eat certain kinds of food.

 3.5 page 176

Possible answers:

1 fast-food restaurants, sit-down restaurants, and street vendors

2 health reasons, religious reasons, to protect animals or the environment, or because they do not like the taste

3 In the United States, regional cuisines include southern, Tex-Mex, Midwestern, and California cuisine.

3.7 page 178

Possible answers:

1 cost, atmosphere, taste, convenience, speed

2 ingredients used, spicy or not, cost, how it is eaten (chopsticks, fork, hands)

3 location, jobs in the business, kind of work involved, goods/services the business offers, profitability of the business

3.8 page 179

Possible answers:

Category 2: Fast-food places

Cost: Fast-food places are usually quite inexpensive.

Convenience: Eating at a fast-food restaurant is very quick and convenient.

Health: Fast food is often not very healthy.

Category 3: Sit-down restaurants

Cost: Sit-down restaurants are usually more expensive than fast-food restaurants.

Convenience: It can take more time to eat at a sit-down restaurant, but it is more convenient than cooking.

Health: A meal at a sit-down restaurant can be very healthy or very unhealthy, depending on the place.

 3.10 page 181

Possible answers:

Body paragraph 1: One type of place that serves food is a street vendor.

Body paragraph 2: Fast-food restaurants are another type of place that serves food.

 3.11 pages 181–182

A

Possible answers:

Category 1: restaurants

Category 2: supermarkets

Category 3: farms

B

Possible answers:

Point of classification A: location

Point of classification B: jobs in the business

Point of classification C: customers

C

Sample paragraph:

    One kind of business that is based on food is a restaurant. Restaurants are common all over the world. In almost every town there is at least one restaurant, and of course in big cities there are thousands of restaurants. There is a wide variety of jobs in a restaurant. Restaurants need chefs and cooks to prepare food, servers to take orders and bring the food, cashiers to take the money, and helpers to clear the tables. In addition, restaurants need managers, cleaning people, and delivery people. The kinds of customers at a restaurant depend on the place. There are restaurants that serve inexpensive food to families as well as very expensive restaurants and restaurants that are mostly for tourists.

 3.12 page 183

Possible answers:

2 The main types of food on a restaurant menu are appetizers, entrees, desserts, and drinks.

3 Where I live, Chinese, Italian, and Mexican are the most popular types of international food.

4 The main types of restaurants in my town are fast-food restaurants, pizza restaurants, and salad places.

4 SHARPEN YOUR SKILLS

Ⓐ Writing Skill: Sentence Variety

page 184

 4.1 page 185

Possible answers:

1 People in China eat hot foods when it is winter. They eat cool foods when it is summer.

2 In many cultures, garlic is considered medicine. It is used to treat colds and other illnesses.

3 In China, many people do not like to drink ice water.

4 Fast food tastes good, but it can be very bad for your health.

B Grammar for Writing: Simple Present and Present Progressive

page 185

 4.3 page 186

1 are enjoying
2 has
3 improves
4 are having
5 are
6 makes
7 do not sleep

Avoiding Common Mistakes   page 187

Another type of diet that is good for your
mental health is a diet high in fish. Scientists are
doing
~~do~~ a lot of research on the effects of fish these
know
days. We already ~~are knowing~~ that fish can
improve memory and concentration, especially for
have
older people. This is because fish ~~are having~~ a fatty
helps
acid called Omega-3 that ~~is helping~~ our brains.
are researching
Right now, scientists ~~research~~ the effect of fish on
people's mood. Many of them believe that fish
suffering
can help people who are ~~suffer~~ from depression.
improves
According to research, fish also ~~is improving~~ sleep.
If you are having trouble sleeping these days, you
might want to try eating more fish for a few days.

C Avoiding Plagiarism   page 188

 4.5 page 189

A
1 b   2 b
B
1 Schlosser, Eric. <u>Fast Food Nation</u>. New York,
   New York: Harper, 1992. Print.
2 Pollan, Michael. "How Change Is Going to
   Come in the Food System." <u>The Nation</u>.
   3 October 2011: 7. Print.

7 PROCESS ESSAYS

SOCIAL WORK: SOCIAL ACTIVISM

page 195

1 *Answers will vary.*
2 *Possible answers:* war, disease, poverty, racism,
   gang violence, pollution, terrorism
3 *Possible answers:* volunteering with an
   organization that addresses social issues, raising
   or donating money to charity, learning about
   an issue and educating other people

1 PREPARE YOUR IDEAS

B Reflect on the Topic   page 196

 1.1 page 196

Step 3. Roll paper strips to make beads.
Step 4. Glue the ends of the beads.
Step 5. String the completed beads.

2 EXPAND YOUR KNOWLEDGE

A Academic Vocabulary   page 198

 2.1 pages 198–199

1 a	3 a	5 b	7 a
2 b	4 b	6 b	8 a

B Academic Collocations   page 199

 2.2 page 199

1 d   2 b   3 a   4 e   5 c

C Writing in the Real World page 200

 2.3 page 201

1 Order of sentences:
1 Raise money and recruit medical professionals.
2 Send a medical team to a country in crisis.
3 Evaluate the country's needs.
4 Provide information and assistance to the country and educate the international community.
5 Give the MSF program to local citizens.
2 *Answers will vary.*
3 *Answers will vary.*

 2.4 page 201

1 *Possible answer:* The writer thinks the work of Doctors Without Borders is very important because it has helped millions of people in crisis situations around the world with its effective and responsible medical and humanitarian aid.
2 The author uses chronological order.
3 The main step of this paragraph is Doctors Without Borders speaking out so that the world community is aware of new problem situations. "Starved for Attention" is an example of this step. It was a campaign that alerted people to the problem of childhood malnutrition and as a result helped starving children.

3 STUDY ACADEMIC WRITING

A Student Model page 202
1 *Possible answer:* This essay will explain how to make a product. Based on the essay title, the product is paper bead jewelry.
2 *Answers will vary.*

Analyze Writing Skills pages 202–203
1 Underlined: The women of Uganda follow a careful step-by-step process to make beads and jewelry.
2 Circled: First, Next, Third, After that, Then, Finally
3 Underlined: This step requires a small stick, such as a toothpick or needle. Roll the paper around the stick very tightly. The stick creates a hole. It is a little difficult to do, so be patient.

4 Circled: In short
Underlined: You can buy paper bead bracelets and necklaces and save yourself time (suggestion); You will have something wonderful and will help the women of Uganda support themselves. (opinion)

 3.1 page 204

1 There are seven steps.
2 b
3 BeadForLife helps women in Uganda. The money provides an income for poor women in Uganda.

 3.2 pages 204–205

I Introductory Paragraph
Thesis Statement: If you follow these steps carefully, perhaps you can make this jewelry, too.
II Body Paragraph
The process of making beads
    Step 1: A. <u>Choose the paper</u>
        Detail: 1. Bright and colorful
        Detail: 2. Magazines or posters
    Step 2: B. Cut the paper
        Detail: 1. <u>Wide and thin triangles</u>
        Detail: 2. Different sizes and shapes
    Step 3: C. Roll the strips into beads
        Detail: 1. Roll paper around a stick or needle
        Detail: 2. <u>Create a hole</u>
    Step 4: D. <u>Glue the paper</u>
        Detail: 1. Hold tightly
        Detail: 2. Wait until dry
    Step 5: E. <u>Make a bracelet</u>
        Detail: 1. Have enough beads
        Detail: 2. Put string through beads
    Step 6: F. <u>Apply varnish</u>
    Step 7: G. Let the beads dry
        Detail: 1. <u>Two to three days</u>
III Concluding Paragraph
Concluding Sentence: In short, making bead jewelry is a simple but long process, and it is a process that the women of Uganda have mastered.

B Process Essays page 206

 3.3 page 206

Introductory Paragraph
1 b   2 c   3 a
Body Paragraph
1 a   2 b
Concluding Paragraph
1 b   2 c   3 a

 3.4 page 207

1 The writer will explain the steps for high school students to start a service-learning project.
2 It is a wonderful opportunity for students to learn important skills, kindness, and responsibility.
3 There are four steps.

 3.6 page 208

Third, roll the paper strips into beads. This step requires a small stick such as a toothpick or needle. Roll the paper around the stick very tightly. The stick creates a hole. It is a little difficult to roll the paper correctly, so be patient. It may take a minute or two to make one bead.

 3.7 page 209

Answers will vary.

 3.9 page 210

1 In sum
2 A bake sale is a quick and easy way to make money to assist people in your community.
3 These kinds of activities will make the people in your community become better neighbors and friends.

 3.10 page 210

In conclusion, if you follow these five easy steps, you can make a delicious soup that will help a sick family member recover quickly. In fact, the soup is so delicious that you will want to serve it to everyone in the family, whether they are sick or not.

4 SHARPEN YOUR SKILLS

A Writing Skill 1: Clarity page 211

 4.1 page 212

Possible answers (relating to the theme):
2 critical   urgent   catastrophic
3 100-person   enormous   tremendous
4 successful   impressive   efficient
5 delicate   attractive   brightly-colored
6 unimportant   tiny   fragile
7 antique   timeless   aged
8 teenage   inexperienced   youthful

 4.2 page 212

Possible answers:
1 teenage or high school
2 successful or valuable
3 an enormous or 100-person
4 attractive or colorful

 4.3 page 213

The TOMS shoe company has the slogan "One for One" on all of its boxes. You might wonder what ~~he~~ *it* means. In fact, this slogan means that you have given a new pair of shoes to a child who does not have any shoes. TOMS makes a commitment to give a pair of shoes away every time a customer buys a new pair of TOMS shoes. TOMS gives ~~him~~ *them* to organizations that have experience working in poor countries or communities. TOMS counts on ~~it~~ *them* to hand out the shoes in an effective way. TOMS has given 10 million pairs of shoes to poor children. The company follows a six-step process. With this process, ~~they~~ *it* provides shoes to children in more than 60 countries. TOMS encourages support from people like you. You can follow these steps to support ~~his~~ *its* "One for One" program.

B Writing Skill 2: Transition Words and Phrases for Sequential Order

page 213

 4.5 page 214

5 On the day of the event, have volunteers register the walkers and hand out water during the walk.

3 After you have a definite location for the walk, find volunteers to help you at the event.

4 Once you have a location and some volunteers, advertise the walking event. Make sure to describe the primary goal of the walk and the time and place of the walk.

1 Choose a place for the walk. A good place for a fundraising walk is a city park.

2 Go to the city government office to get permission for your event.

Sample paragraph:

Charity organizations often use walks or runs to raise money. Anyone can use this popular fundraising idea by following these steps. First, choose a place for the walk. A good place for a fundraising walk is a city park. Next, go to the city government office to get permission for your event. Then after you have a definite location for the walk, find volunteers to help you at the event. Fourth, once you have a location and some volunteers, advertise the walking event. Make sure to describe the primary goal of the walks and the time and place of the walk. Finally, on the day of the event, have volunteers register the walkers and hand out water during the walk.

C Grammar for Writing: Phrasal Verbs page 214

 4.6 page 216

1 find out   4 count on
2 sign up   5 hand out
3 fill out

Avoiding Common Mistakes page 217

 4.7 page 217

First, decide the date and location for your blood drive. You need to work with the Red Cross to choose a date when they are available. Also, find out ~~know~~ how much space the Red Cross requires for their equipment. Find out ~~Learn~~ if your location will work well. After that, you can begin advertising the event. The Red Cross recommends that you begin advertising four weeks before the event. At the same time, you can sign up ~~subscribe~~ donors. Sign people up ~~in~~ to give blood and schedule appointments. On the day of the event, call donors to remind them of their appointment times. Next, greet the Red Cross workers and show them where to set up. When donors arrive, the Red Cross staff will do everything. They help donors fill out ~~write~~ the necessary paperwork. After all the paperwork is filled out ~~answered~~, the staff safely takes the blood donations. Finally, find out ~~check~~ how many people gave blood so that you can announce the results and thank all of the donors.

C Avoiding Plagiarism page 218

 4.8 page 219

1 a   2 b   3 a, c

8 COMPARISON AND CONTRAST ESSAYS

FINANCE: PERSONAL FINANCE

page 223
Answers will vary.

1 PREPARE YOUR IDEAS

B Reflect on the Topic page 224

ACTIVITY 1.1 page 224

Possible answers:
- Studying full-time – more free time
- Similarities – students can make new friends
- Studying part-time while working – less choice of classes per semester

2 EXPAND YOUR KNOWLEDGE

A Academic Vocabulary page 226

ACTIVITY 2.1 page 226

A
1 b   2 d   3 c   4 a
B
1 d   2 b   3 a   4 c

B Academic Phrases page 227

ACTIVITY 2.2 page 227

1 c   2 a   3 b

C Writing in the Real World page 228

ACTIVITY 2.3 page 229

1 The generations differ in their use of technology. Gen Y uses technology to stay connected with friends and family on social media. They use social media to see what their friends and peers are buying. Gen X uses technology to search for information. They use this information to inform their choice of purchases.
2 *Answers will vary.*
3 *Possible answers:* Gen X will need a lot of product information. The company could put information about the material, colors, sizes, prices, and care on their website for Gen X. Gen Y will want to know what other people think of the jeans. The company could have advertisements on social media that people can "like" and "share." They could create an ad campaign in which people take pictures of themselves wearing the jeans and post them on social media.

ACTIVITY 2.4 page 229

1 The purpose of this information is to provide interest and to give some background information. The paragraph provides a specific example of an advertisement that targets Millennials.
2 The author is comparing Gen X and Gen Y. He is comparing their use of technology.
3 The author discusses the spending habits of both Gen X and Gen Y.

3 STUDY ACADEMIC WRITING

A Student Model page 230

1 The prompt is asking the writer to compare students who study full-time and students who work and study part-time.
2 *Answers will vary.*
Possible similarities: Both students take the same courses; they do the same work; they get a college education.
Possible differences: Full-time students can take more courses at a time; they have more time to get the work done; they usually graduate sooner because they can take more courses at once.

Analyze Writing Skills pages 230–231

1 Underlined: How long will it take to get a degree? How much will it cost?
2 Circled: study full-time, study part-time
3 Underlined: students will have different experiences, will graduate at different times, and will have different amounts of debt after graduation
4 Circled: Paragraph 2: (different) experiences
Paragraph 3: time (that it takes to graduate)
Paragraph 4: debt (after graduation)
The writer discusses both.
5 Underlined: In conclusion

 3.1 page 232

1 The differences are experiences, time, and debt.
2 The writer discovered that in his case it was better to work while going to school. Someone trying to decide how to pay for college might benefit from this essay.
3 *Answers will vary.*

 3.2 pages 232–234

I Introductory Paragraph
Thesis Statement: Studying full-time and part-time are different because students will have different experiences, will graduate at different times, and will have different amounts of debt after graduation.

Body Paragraph 1
II Student experience
    Subject A: A. Full-time students
        Detail: 1. Enjoy college life
            Sub-detail: a. Take classes anytime
            Sub-detail: b. Meet people
            Sub-detail: c. Participate in organizations
    Subject B: B. Part-time students
        Detail: 1. Don't enjoy college life very much
            Sub-detail: a. Very busy working
            Sub-detail: b. Don't socialize as much
            Sub-detail: c. No time for school organization

Body Paragraph 2
III Time to graduate
    Subject A: A. Full-time students
        Detail: 1. Graduate on time
            Sub-detail: a. Take many classes
            Sub-detail: b. Finish quickly
    Subject B: B. Part-time students
        Detail: 1. Go to school longer
            Sub-detail: a. Take fewer classes
            Sub-detail: b. Need time to work

Body Paragraph 3
IV Debt after graduation
    Subject A: A. Full-time students
        Detail: 1. Have debt
            Sub-detail: a. Need to repay loans
            Sub-detail: b. Often have financial problems
    Subject B: B. Part-time students
        Detail: 1. Less debt
            Sub-detail: a. No loans to repay
            Sub-detail: b. Often can start a family earlier
            Sub-detail: c. Can make big purchases sooner

V Concluding Paragraph
Concluding Sentence: In conclusion, studying full-time and studying part-time are different in many important ways.

B Comparison and Contrast Essays page 234

 3.3 page 235

1 a   2 b   3 b   4 b   5 a

 3.4 page 236

Possible answers:

Points of Comparison	Subject A: Shopping in a Store	Subject B: Shopping Online
Body Paragraph 2: shipping and handling	usually no shipping costs	often have extra shipping and handling costs
Body Paragraph 3: getting the best price	can compare by going to different stores	can compare by going to different websites

ACTIVITY 3.6 page 237

A

What makes a person a saver instead of a spender? Psychologists continue to debate the factors that determine personality. Some experts argue that genetics decides our behaviors and attitudes. Others say that it is mainly environment that affects who we become. My brother and I have the same parents, but we grew up very differently. He grew up in the 1980s when our parents were poor, but I grew up in the 1990s when our family had a higher income. It is clear that this difference in our environments as children caused my brother and me to view money differently.

B

1 a

2 a

3 It is clear that this difference in our environments as children caused my brother and me to view money differently; b

 ACTIVITY 3.7 page 238

1 Focusing on similarities and differences between cash and credit cards can help people decide which payment option is safer. (The other statement does not include the key characteristic of safety.)

2 Shopping at local stores and shopping at large national chain stores have some clear differences that consumers should consider when deciding where to buy products. (The other statement does not introduce a comparison of local vs. global shopping.)

 ACTIVITY 3.8 page 239

Possible answers:

2 get a college education

3 how we spend money

 ACTIVITY 3.10 page 240

Possible answers:

Body Paragraph 1: Changing their menus

A Wendy's
  1 new item: Pretzel Bacon Cheeseburger
  2 "fast-casual" vs. fast-food

B KFC
  1 new item: all boneless wings
  2 attract Millennials who grew up with chicken nuggets

ACTIVITY 3.11 page 241

Possible answers:

1 Topic sentence for body paragraph 2:
Another similarity between online banking and traditional banking is the type of accounts that customers can have.
Topic sentence for body paragraph 3:
Finally, traditional banking is the same as online banking because they both offer the same interest rates.

2 Topic sentence for body paragraph 1:
The most important difference between shopping online and traditional shopping is the type of interaction customers have with the products.
Topic sentence for body paragraph 2:
Another difference is the type of information consumers can get about the product.
Topic sentence for body paragraph 3:
The last difference between shopping online and traditional shopping is the amount and type of interaction customers have with the sales staff.

 ACTIVITY 3.12 page 241

Answers will vary.

 ACTIVITY 3.13 page 242

1 b   2 c   3 a

4 SHARPEN YOUR SKILLS

A Writing Skill: Hooks page 243

 ACTIVITY 4.1 page 243

Writing in the Real World: 2 – a relevant short story
Student Model: 4 – a significant question or two

 ACTIVITY 4.2 page 244

A

1 Underlined: "An iPod, a phone, an Internet mobile communicator … these are NOT three separate devices! And we are calling it iPhone!"

2 d

3 *Answers will vary.*

B

Answers will vary.

B Grammar for Writing: Comparative Adjectives page 245

 4.4 page 246

1 healthier than
2 faster than
3 more common than
4 better than, smaller than
5 more successful than

Avoiding Common Mistakes page 247

 4.5 page 247

The most important difference between using a credit card and using cash is that cash is ~~more harder~~ *harder* to spend than credit cards. For that reason, many financial advisors argue that using cash is ~~more better~~ *better* than using credit cards. Experts have found that shoppers make more purchases when they use credit cards. There is a psychological reason for this. It is ~~more easy~~ *easier* to swipe a credit card to buy something. This action does not make people feel like they are spending money. On the other hand, studies show that people who use cash spend less. Cash feels more real ~~that~~ *than* credit cards, so people treat it differently. Most people try to keep cash. They find cash more difficult to use ~~that~~ *than* credit. People who are trying to save money may find that using cash is ~~helpful~~ *more helpful* than using credit cards.

C Avoiding Plagiarism page 248

 4.6 page 249

1 change the order of words
2 change words or phrases to synonyms
3 change the form of words

 4.7 page 249

Answers will vary.

NAME: ....

DATE: ....

Part A: Academic Vocabulary

Circle the correct words to complete the sentences.

1 It takes many years to **sharpen / master / criticize** a second language.

2 Children must recognize and say the sounds of letters. These skills are **mental / able / critical** for learning how to read.

3 To do well in college, it is important to pay **technique / ability /attention** to class lectures and take good notes.

4 One way to learn new words in a language is to **sharpen / memorize / attend** songs. When you sing a song over and over, you learn the words in it.

5 People who **sharpen / master / memorize** their minds usually do well when they have to learn new skills at a job.

6 According to research studies, video games can improve children's **technique / ability / attention** to read.

7 Connecting new vocabulary words to familiar words is one **ability / technique / attention** for remembering the new words.

8 Solving crossword puzzles can help people's **mental / sharp / memorizable** ability because it requires clear thinking.

Part B: Academic Collocations

Complete the paragraph with the correct form of the academic collocations in the box.

attention span	learning technique	memory loss	mental health	pay attention

Two very different brain conditions show the brain's critical importance. The first is Attention Deficit Hyperactivity Disorder (ADHD), which is especially common in children. Children with ADHD have trouble sitting still for very long. They often cannot .... in class. They may listen for a few
(1)
minutes, but then they move around and talk. Their .... are very short.
(2)
One .... for children with ADHD is to study things in short chunks. The second
(3)
condition is Alzheimer's, which mostly affects older people. People with Alzheimer's have serious

.... They often cannot remember events and people, and they may even forget their
(4)
own children. In sum, problems with the brain can cause serious difficulties in people's lives, so it's important

to take care of one's ....
(5)

NAME: ....

DATE: ....

Part A

Circle the correct words to complete the sentences.

1 I began practicing yoga **even though / because** I felt stressed from my busy schedule.

2 **Although / Since** Julia sleeps eight hours a night, she still has trouble focusing on her studies.

3 Cooking with family and friends is beneficial **since / , although** it helps people connect socially.

4 **While / Since** children should avoid most computer games, some educational computer games may actually help children learn.

5 Some people don't eat healthy food such as fruit and vegetables, **even though / since** doctors highly recommend it.

6 I study more efficiently after exercising **because / although** I feel more energetic.

Part B

Correct the mistakes with adverb clauses.

1 Although teenagers can be moody, their behavior usually improves as they get older.

2 Reading an enjoyable book before bed is healthy, because it relaxes you.

3 Even though Professor Lu never gives us homework on weekends to relieve our stress. I usually study anyway.

4 I am thinking more clearly. Since I began doing challenging crossword puzzles.

5 Although it's a good idea to avoid a lot of caffeine, and some people say it helps them stay alert.

NAME: ....

DATE: ....

Part A

Read the original passage and the underlined words and phrases in the student texts below.
Circle the type of plagiarism in each student text.

Original Passage:

A mnemonic is a technique people use to remember something. It can be an abbreviation, such as an acronym, or an image, such as a bird. It can also be a song or poem. Using mnemonics can help people remember things such as people's names, numbers, or facts. For example, when you meet someone at a party named Elizabeth, you can think of Queen Elizabeth of England. For another example, if students are studying historical facts for a test, they can remember them as a poem: "In 1492, Columbus sailed the ocean blue."

1 **Student Text A:**

To help <u>remember something</u>, use a <u>mnemonic technique</u> such as an <u>abbreviation, an image, a song, or a poem</u>. You can use a mnemonic to remember names, number, or facts. If <u>you meet someone</u> with the name <u>Elizabeth</u>, for example, <u>think of Queen Elizabeth of England</u>.

a This student cut and pasted whole sentences.

b This student only changed a few words.

2 **Student Text B:**

<u>A mnemonic is a technique people use to remember something. It can be an abbreviation, such as an acronym, or an image, such as a bird. It can also be a song or poem. Using mnemonics can help people remember things such as people's names, numbers, or facts.</u> It can be fun to create clever poems or songs with a study friend.

a This student cut and pasted whole sentences.

b This student only changed a few words.

(CONTINUED)

Part B

Read the original passage and the examples of plagiarism in two students' texts below.
Underline the phrases that the students plagiarized.

Original Passage:

Creativity is the ability to think of new ideas or make something original or innovative. Nowadays, creativity is encouraged in schools to promote original, individual thinking. It also allows students to think of new approaches to problem solving. This is especially useful not only in art classes, but also in science and technology classes.

1 **Student Text A:**

Creativity, or the ability to think of new ideas or make something original or innovative, is used in schools. Students can learn to solve problems in a fun way, not only in art classes but also in science and technology classes.

2 **Student Text B:**

Creativity means making new or innovative ideas or things. This method is encouraged in schools to promote original, individual thinking. Students will be able to use new approaches to problem solving. This is very helpful when they learn about a variety of subjects including science, technology, and the arts.

NAME: ....   DATE: ....

Instructors: This is a list of possible prompts to assign as a unit writing quiz.

1 What three things can you do in class to help you remember better? Explain and give examples.

2 What strategies do you use to help you remember new vocabulary?

3 The brain needs sleep to work well. How can people improve their habits to sleep better?

4 What three strategies can you use to study for a test? Explain and give examples.

5 What strategies can you use to remember people's names? Give details.

NAME: .... DATE: ....

Part A: Academic Vocabulary

Circle the correct words to complete the sentences.

1 In the U.S, it is considered **brief / respectful / cultural** for children to use "Mr.," "Mrs.," or "Ms." before an adult's last name when talking to him or her.

2 Most Americans **avoid / communicate / interpret** talking about religion and politics with strangers. These topics could make them feel uncomfortable.

3 Many Americans **communicate / avoid / regard** a hug as an appropriate gesture with family and friends. However, it is generally not appropriate with strangers.

4 In some cultures, a thumbs-up gesture means "good job." In other cultures, people **avoid / interpret / respect** this gesture as having a rude meaning.

5 People in many cultures **communicate / avoid / interpret** nonverbally with hand and head gestures.

6 A **custom / culture / respect** in many cultures is to greet family and friends with a kiss on the cheek.

7 In many **communications / respects / cultures** throughout the world, people greet each other with a handshake or a wave.

8 In Japan, a **brief / cultural / respectful** bow of the head is used when greeting friends, but a deeper bow is expected when meeting someone for the first time.

Part B: Academic Phrases

Complete the paragraph with the academic phrases in the box.

another	a number of	one of the

For students who are studying a new language, being polite can help them learn the language.

In fact, there are .... benefits that learning etiquette can have for students.
(1)

.... benefits of knowing social rules is a better understanding of the culture.
(2)

When people understand the culture of the target language, it becomes easier to understand vocabulary

and idioms. .... benefit of learning etiquette is that it helps students feel more
(3)

comfortable with native speakers. For example, if students know to shake hands and smile when they greet

strangers, it will be easier for them to meet people. In short, knowing the social rules helps students to feel

more comfortable speaking a new language.

NAME: .... DATE: ....

Part A

Circle the correct words or phrases to complete the sentences.

1 At dinner parties in **some / a little** countries, it is the custom to wait until the host sits down before starting to eat.

2 American dinner guests usually bring flowers or chocolates to a dinner party. A **few of / few** these guests might bring a special gift for the host.

3 There are still **a little / a few** Chinese customs that I need to learn about before I go to Beijing.

4 The **amount of / number of** Americans who know a second language is increasing.

5 There is **little / few** instruction provided to foreign students about some complex aspects of American culture.

6 You can find **a large amount of / many of** information about customs in different cultures on the Internet.

Part B

Correct the mistake in each sentence.

1 Most Americans try to leave little space between themselves and strangers.

2 Today there is a large number of online communication across cultures.

3 Few of residents of San Francisco have never been to the city's famous Chinatown.

4 People who are moving to a new country can learn about the culture by reading a lot books.

5 Little gesture such as a smile can help people make friends in a new culture.

NAME: ....   DATE: ....

Match each scenario with the best strategy for avoiding plagiarism.

SCENARIO

.... 1 Sam says that authorities on his topic write better than he does, so he plans to copy the experts' words.

.... 2 Sherry says she doesn't know the specific vocabulary for her topic, and her dictionary doesn't seem to help.

.... 3 Isabella was confident that she could write her paper the night before it is due. Now it is due tomorrow and she doesn't know what to write about.

STRATEGY

a Ask a teacher, a classmate, or a librarian for help.

b Organize time by starting the writing project early and doing some of it every day.

c Remember that copying is always wrong, and it is against the school's academic integrity policy.

NAME: ....   DATE: ....

Instructors: This is a list of possible prompts to assign as a unit writing quiz.

1 What gestures and body language do friends use with each other but not with strangers?

2 Choose a country you know well. Describe the nonverbal behavior that family members use with each other.

3 What nonverbal greetings for hello and goodbye do people use in a country you know well? Explain and give examples.

4 Describe the etiquette for classroom behavior in a country you know well.

5 Explain the etiquette for eating a meal in a country you know well.

NAME: ....   DATE: ....

Part A: Academic Vocabulary

Circle the correct words to complete the sentences.

1 Immigrants often **struggle / reveal / identify** to feel at home in their new country.

2 Ireland's national **concern / acceptance / identity** became stronger when it gained independence from Great Britain.

3 The statues in the national monument **accept / reveal / struggle** important people in the country's history.

4 Many countries are proud of their **social / ethnic / acceptable** programs, such as paid health care and affordable education.

5 Some countries show great **identity / struggle / concern** for their poor by providing housing, food, and work opportunities.

6 Singapore is proud of its many **social / ethnic / acceptable** groups, such as Chinese, Malaysian, and Indian.

7 Many citizens of the United States think it is **acceptable / ethnic / social** for foreign residents to speak their own language, as long as they learn English.

8 After Anthony lived in Switzerland for six months, he gained a better understanding of the country's **concerns / values / struggles**, such as peace, fairness, and punctuality.

Part B: Academic Collocations

Complete the sentences with the academic collocations in the box.

ethnic background	ethnic groups	national identity	social class	social values

1 Many Americans show their .... on the Fourth of July by displaying the American flag.

2 In some countries, ... does not affect success. Even the poorest people can become highly successful.

3 Freedom of speech and equality are important American ....

4 Cubans, Haitians, and Bahamians are just some of the .... that live in Miami.

5 Michael has an interesting .... His mother is part Filipino and part German, and his father is African American.

NAME: ....   DATE: ....

Part A

Circle the correct words to complete the sentences.

1 The Great Wall of China is one of the great **China / Chinese** accomplishments.

2 One of the most **relaxing / relaxed** trips is to take a boat ride down Germany's historic Rhine River.

3 Southern **Italian / Italy** is known for its pizza and pasta.

4 Most first-time visitors to the Grand Canyon in Arizona are **amazing / amazed** when they see one of the U.S.'s most treasured natural sites .

5 The **Mexican / Mexico** holiday Cinco de Mayo is also celebrated in many communities in the United States.

6 Since Debbie is **interesting / interested** in the theater, she plans to visit the Old Globe Theater when she visits London next summer.

7 It was **shocking / shocked** for the visitors to see wild alligators up close in Florida's Everglades National Park.

8 **Australias / Australians** are quite proud of the Great Barrier Reef that sits off their northeast coast.

Part B

Correct the seven mistakes in the paragraph. There is one mistake in each sentence.

(1) If you are interesting in seeing a historic American city, I recommend you visit Boston, Massachusetts. (2) There are many excite things to do, such as walking along the historic Freedom Trail, visiting the Public Garden, and taking a ride on the Swan Boats. (3) You'll find that Boston has an international flair: the South Boston neighborhood is an irish neighborhood, where you'll find restaurants typical of that country. (4) If you want Korea food, be sure to visit Allston Village. (5) Italy food is abundant in the city's historic North End. (6) Don't be confusing by the city's old streets – buy a local map and you will have no trouble getting around. (7) Finally, the museums are not to be missed: the Museum of Fine Arts, the New England Aquarium, and the Museum of Science are all fascinated.

NAME: ....

DATE: ....

Part A

Check (✓) the information that is common knowledge.

- [ ] 1 Statistics about population
- [ ] 2 A description of your city's neighborhoods
- [ ] 3 Holiday traditions
- [ ] 4 Government information about migration
- [ ] 5 A university professor's research on your topic
- [ ] 6 Your opinion
- [ ] 7 Common historical facts
- [ ] 8 Common current topics of discussion

Part B

Why are the sentences below NOT common knowledge? Write R if the information is from research or O if it another person's opinion.

.... 1 Professor Luis Garcia states that fewer Colombians are practicing Catholicism today.

.... 2 Mardi Gras was first made a holiday in 1582.

.... 3 The first Mardi Gras celebration in the U.S. happened on March 3, 1699.

.... 4 Zhang Lu says there are many interesting multicultural celebrations in Beijing.

.... 5 Guy Fawkes Day is a typical British holiday, according to a British history blog.

.... 6 In 2013, there were 7.8 million immigrants in the United Kingdom, making it truly multicultural.

.... 7 Every year, more that 6 million people go to Germany's famous Oktoberfest.

NAME: ....   **DATE:** ....

Instructors: This is a list of possible prompts to assign as a unit writing quiz.

1   Describe a coin or bill from a country you know well. Explain the meaning of the images, words, or symbols on the currency.

2   Describe a famous painting or photograph from a country you know well.

3   Describe a tradition that your family celebrates. Describe how it symbolizes your family's social, national, or cultural values.

4   Think of a country's national flag. Describe the shape, design, and colors of the flag. Explain how it symbolizes the country's national identity.

5   Describe a famous monument or a statue in a country you know well. Explain what it looks like and what it symbolizes.

NAME: ....

DATE: ....

Part A: Academic Vocabulary

Circle the correct words to complete the paragraph.

Casual Friday is a day when office workers can wear less formal clothes than usual. They do not have to

wear suits and dresses. Usually the company has more **habit / control / conflict** over what employees wear,
(1)

but on Fridays employees have more choice. However, Casual Fridays can sometimes be a problem. Some

employees do not understand the company **conflicts / controls / policies** about Casual Friday. They wear
(2)

clothes that are too informal, such as shorts and jeans. They cannot **request / behave / distinguish**
(3)

between appropriate and inappropriate clothes. Some companies don't want casual clothes to become

a **control / habit / request**. They are afraid employees will wear jeans all week instead of just on Fridays.
(4)

In addition, some employees **distinguish / behave / encourage** too casually on Casual Fridays. They take
(5)

long lunches or leave early and do not do much work. If employees want to leave early on Friday, they need

to **request / distinguish / behave** time off. If a company needs employees to work but they leave early,
(6)

it can lead to a **control / conflict / policy**. Most often, however, employees follow the rules because
(7)

they know that Casual Friday rewards workers. The policy **encourages / behaves / distinguishes** employees
(8)

to stay with the company.

Part B: Academic Phrases

Complete the paragraph with the correct form of the academic phrases in the box.

a kind of	in other words	be related to

"Water-cooler talk" is .... workplace conversation about office news and gossip.
(1)

This kind of conversation .... "small talk," that is, conversation about the weather,
(2)

sports, or news, because they are both informal. In addition, water-cooler talk often includes topics about

people's personal lives. ...., people talk about their families and social lives.
(3)

NAME: ....   DATE: ....

Part A

Label the underlined nouns and pronouns in each sentence CS (count-singular), CP (count-plural), or NC (noncount).

1 A good <u>manager</u> offers <u>employees</u> a lot of <u>encouragement</u>.

2 Many <u>companies</u> provide <u>information</u> about their <u>benefits</u> on an internal <u>website</u>.

3 Professional <u>behavior</u> is expected at the <u>office</u>, but at office <u>parties</u> <u>employees</u> can relax.

4 My <u>boss</u> is strict about <u>etiquette</u> in work-related <u>emails</u>.

5 <u>Stefano</u> was happy to share his <u>knowledge</u> about the <u>organization</u> with the new <u>employee</u>.

6 Open <u>communication</u> is necessary if <u>you</u> want to work well with your <u>colleagues</u>.

Part B

Circle the correct words or phrases to complete the sentences.

1 Our new manager is very good at providing **encouragement / encouragements** to new employees.

2 It's **a good idea / good idea** to stay informed about one's field of work.

3 Even if employees get angry at their boss, they must show **control / a control** in their emotions at work.

4 **Many / Much** education is necessary to become a lawyer or doctor.

5 A lot of information **are / is** available on how to use the latest technology at work.

6 The accounting manager eats lunch with **colleague / a colleague** in the company's cafeteria every day.

NAME: ....   DATE: ....

Part A

Check (✓) the good sources to use in a paragraph about communication skills at work.

☐ 1 an article by a professor in a university's business program

☐ 2 a *New York Times* article on successful communication strategies

☐ 3 a talk with a friend who works at another company

☐ 4 a blog written by a business manager

☐ 5 a government journal on recent workplace policies

Part B

Read each scenario. Circle the source the student should use.

1 Kim wants to write a paragraph on what it means to be a good leader. She should use information from:

   a an article from the website *become-a-leader.com*.

   b a Harvard Business School case study on leadership.

2 Cameron is writing a paragraph on the definition of responsibility at work. He should use information from:

   a an article from the City of San Francisco's business administration department.

   b an informal handbook written by an employee of a large company.

3 Stefan wants to write a paragraph on balancing family and work life. He should use information from:

   a a newsletter by women who stay at home to care for children.

   b a Pew Research Center study on the effects working parents have on children.

NAME: .... DATE: ....

Instructors: This is a list of possible prompts to assign as a unit writing quiz.

1 Write a definition of *success* from your point of view. Give examples.

2 Write a definition of *cooperation*. What does it mean in the workplace of a country you know well? Give examples.

3 The expression "the early bird catches the worm" means that if a person does a task immediately, he or she will succeed. Explain how this expression applies to the workplace.

4 What is your definition of a good boss? Explain.

5 Define *responsibility*. Explain how it applies to both employers and employees.

NAME: ....   DATE: ....

Part A: Academic Vocabulary

Circle the correct words to complete the paragraph.

Creativity is an important **range / concept / exploration** in our society. In fact, there is a clear
(1)

need for humans to **create / motivate / range** art, movies, and books. We also always need people to
(2)

motivate / relate / design new consumer items such as furniture and clothing. However, I think it is
(3)

a bad idea to have more TV programs about the arts. These programs lose money. Earning big profits

explores / motivates / designs most television channels to stay away from arts programming. They cannot
(4)

show a program unless it is **capable / relevant / explored** of making money from advertisements. They can
(5)

only show programs that a lot of people will want to watch. In the past, TV station staff have done research

on their viewers to **concept / explore / range** ideas for new programs. They learned that TV viewers are
(6)

only interested in a small **range / concept / capability** of shows: sitcoms, dramas, reality shows, and sports.
(7)

Programs about painting, opera, or ballet are not **capable / designed / relevant** to them. In sum, we cannot
(8)

expect TV stations to spend money on programs that will not be popular.

Part B: Academic Collocations

Complete the sentences with the correct form of the academic collocations in the box.

basic concept	capable of expressing	explore the possibility	main motivation	a wide range of

Artists usually do not earn much money. Therefore, they should .... of using
(1)

their art in other professions. Everyone knows the saying, "Money does not buy happiness." This is a

.... that we all understand. It means that if your .... in life is to
(2)   (3)

be rich, you might achieve that goal; however, you still may not be very happy. However, people must still

make enough money to live. Luckily, there is .... jobs for artists in advertising, movie
(4)

production design, webpage design, and book illustration. Artists who are .... their
(5)

creative ideas would do especially well in any of these jobs. In fact, artists who choose one of these careers

can be creative and have enough money to live.

NAME: .... DATE: ....

Part A

Complete the sentences with the correct forms of the word in parentheses.

1 After Anjali finished her art program in high school, she reached the .... that she
   .... (conclude)
   wanted to major in art therapy.

2 Design thinking, or using .... to solve problems, is a new educational approach in
   (create)
   many schools today.

3 Judith was happy about her .... when the audience cheered loudly.
   (perform)

4 The dance students .... learned the new, exciting dance routine.
   (happy)

5 Some schools have shown the .... of teaching art in school by offering art classes
   (important)
   to parents, too.

6 The teachers played an .... role in helping their students think creatively.
   (active)

Part B

Correct the mistakes in the paragraph. There is one mistake in each sentence.

(1) Parents should encourage their children to draw and paint at home because they will see the differance
in their children's performance at school. (2) Creative can help children think clearly, therefore do better
in their classes. (3) Self-confidance is another benefit of encouraging the arts at home because children
generally feel good about their creations. (4) In addition, if they see their own artwork on display, it can be
a powerfull way to make them feel confident. (5) This is especialy true for shy children. (6) Final, one of the
best benefits is that parents can create art along with their children. (7) This can make a big different in how
children feel about art.

NAME: ....

DATE: ....

Part A

Read the original quote. Then match each student citation with the citation strategy that the student used.

Original Quote:

"A current observation in the field of arts education is there are two overall trends, both powerful and yet contradictory. On the one hand, arts educators are struggling to maintain their tenuous foothold in the classroom in the wake of the movement for higher academic standards in other subjects, testing requirements, and budget cuts. On the other hand, there is a growing and compelling body of research illustrating the benefits of arts education for students and schools …"

Source: "Education Leaders Institute Alumni Summit Report." *National Endowment for the Arts.* April 2014. p. 3. Web. 4 May 2015.

Student Citation

.... 1 According to the Education Leaders Institute Alumni Summit Report of the National Endowment of the Arts, there are currently two trends in art education. In one, art teachers are competing with smaller budgets. In the other arts education is shown to have many benefits on students. (3).

.... 2 Arts education is divided into two groups nowadays: one favors arts in schools, and the other favors giving more money to other academic programs. (National Endowment for the Arts ELI Summit Report 3).

.... 3 In the recent National Endowment for the Arts Education Leaders Institute Report, "On the other hand, there is a growing and compelling body of research illustrating the benefits of arts education for students and schools …" (3).

Citation Strategy

a The student put the author's exact words in quotation marks.

b The student put the author's ideas in his own words and used the author's name in the sentence with a signal phrase (an in-text citation).

c The student put the author's ideas in her own words and cited the author's name at the end of the sentence.

(CONTINUED)

Part B

Read the original passage and a paragraph from a student's essay. Check (✓) the two citation strategies the student used.

Original Passage:

"The internet and social media are integral to the arts in America. A survey of arts organizations that have received grants from the National Endowment for the Arts (NEA) finds that technology use permeates these organizations, their marketing and education efforts, and even their performance offerings. Moreover, many organizations are using the internet and social media to expand the number of online performances and exhibits, grow their audience, sell tickets, and raise funds online, while allowing patrons to share content, leave comments, and even post their own content on organizations' sites."

Source: Thomas, Kristin, et al. "Arts Organizations and Digital Technologies." Pew Research Center. 4 Jan 2013. Web. 4 May 2015.

Paragraph from Student's Essay:

Many think the arts and technology are not able to work together. They seem to come from opposite places – organic creativity, and industrial-age innovation. However, according to Kristin Thomas, in her article "Arts Organizations and Digital Technologies," arts organizations indeed use technology in education and marketing. In fact, the author states, "many organizations are using the internet and social media to expand the number of online performances and exhibits, grow their audience, sell tickets, and raise funds online, while allowing patrons to share content, leave comments, and even post their own content on organizations' sites (1)." It seems clear that arts and technology are indeed naturally connected.

1 The student put the author's exact words in quotation marks.

2 The student put the author's ideas in his own words and used the author's name in the sentence with a signal phrase (an in-text citation).

3 The student put the author's ideas in his own words and cited the author's name at the end of the sentence.

NAME: .... **DATE:** ....

Instructors: This is a list of possible prompts to assign as a unit writing quiz.

1 Do you think community colleges should offer free art classes to adults? Explain.

2 Because of limited money, some high schools have stopped offering arts classes so they can have more academic classes such as math and science. Do you agree or disagree with this decision? Explain.

3 Should art museums charge entrance fees or allow people to enter for free? Explain.

4 Is it important to expose young children to art in school? Explain.

5 Some communities have street fairs showing local artists' work. They close city streets to have these fairs. Do you think these fairs should occur in the street or elsewhere? Explain.

NAME: ....

DATE: ....

Part A: Academic Vocabulary

Circle the correct words to complete the sentences.

1 In Spain, it is **medical / conditional / traditional** to eat 12 grapes at midnight on New Year's Eve for good luck.

2 Some very old food customs are still an important part of **contemporary / medical / conditional** life today.

3 One **condition / approach / medicine** to losing weight is to eat until you are no longer hungry, but not full.

4 Some people believe that chicken soup is as good as **medicine / treatment / approach** for fighting colds.

5 Some societies believe a special kind of tea can **approach / condition / treat** serious illnesses.

6 If a person has a **condition / medicine / treatment** such as an allergy, he or she cannot eat certain foods.

7 People with food allergies must **treat / medicate / eliminate** the problem foods from their diets.

8 People who **eliminate / suffer / treat** from high blood pressure or heart disease have to be extremely careful about the amount of salt in restaurant food.

Part B: Academic Phrases

Complete the paragraph with the academic phrases in the box.

appears to be	it is possible	a variety of

In family farms in the U.S., most of the work is done by the owners and their children or relatives. These small farms produce .... food, including corn, eggs, milk, fruit, and vegetables.
(1)
The families often sell this food to local customers. If you live in a city, ... to buy food
(2)
from family farms by shopping at farmers' markets – small markets that sell food from local farms. In recent years, it has become more difficult for a small family farm to succeed. As a result, the number of family farms in the U.S. .... decreasing.
(3)

NAME: .... DATE: ....

Part A

Complete the sentences with the simple present or present progressive form of the verb in parentheses.

1 Recipe websites .... even the worst cooks good ideas for meals.
  (give)

2 Tara .... only natural foods for three weeks because she is on a special diet.
  (eat)

3 Most supermarkets nowadays .... organic produce.
  (have)

4 Some people .... sugar from their diet now because they think it is unhealthy.
  (eliminate)

5 Even though tofu .... plain, it is delicious when spices are added.
  (taste)

6 Marco and Rosa .... fruit and vegetables at farmer's market today.
  (sell)

7 Professor Martin .... of teaching a course in nutrition and mental health
  (think)
  next semester.

8 The Eden Café .... both vegetarian and non-vegetarian food every day.
  (serve)

Part B

Circle the correct words or phrases to complete the paragraph.

Food waste is a growing problem in the United States. It **comes / is coming** from three main sources.
(1)
First, supermarkets **throw / are throwing** away perfectly good food every day. For example, if cans are
(2)
slightly damaged, a supermarket will throw them away. Another source of food waste is from restaurants.
Often restaurants **buy / are buying** food that they don't cook so the food is wasted. The third main source of
(3)
food waste is from consumers. When people buy food, they usually plan to eat it. However, they often
toss / are tossing it in the garbage if they don't eat it right away. Now, many communities **try / are trying**
(4)   (5)
to find a way to stop food waste. In fact, some communities **seem / are seeming** ready to solve this
(6)
problem. For example, this month my community **organizes / is organizing** a food drive for the homeless.
(7)
Many people **believe / are believing** if their communities organize similar events, food waste can be a thing
(8)
of the past.

NAME: ....

DATE: ....

Part A

Read each in-text citation for information from a printed source. Circle the letter of the missing information.

1 Food expert Shea McGrath recommends that people support their local farmers to improve both their health and the local economy.

   a date

   b author's name

   c page number

2 "Good food can be both healthy and enjoyable to eat." (76).

   a author's name

   b page number

   c publisher

3 In his book, he states that visiting the weekly farmers' market can also lead to a stronger sense of community because it makes neighborhood residents feel good about where they live. (92).

   a signal phrase

   b author's name

   c page number

Part B

Read the works-cited entries for printed sources. Circle the letter of the error in each entry.

1 **Book:**
   Gillian Crowther. *Eating Culture: An Anthropological Guide to Food.* Toronto: University of Toronto Press, 2013. Print.

   a The title of the book should be in quotes.

   b The author's last name should appear first.

   c The name of the publisher should appear before the city.

2 **Magazine:**
   Shockey, Kristin. "Eat More Kraut." *Taproot Magazine.* 2014: 45. Print.

   a The title of the article should be italicized.

   b The page number should not be included.

   c The date should include the month, day, and year.

3 **Newspaper:**
   Druckerman, Pamela. "Eat Up. You'll Be Happier." *The New York Times.* 23 April 2015: A27. Print.

   a The title of the article should be italicized.

   b The author's full name should be listed.

   c The page number should not be included.

NAME: .... **DATE:** ....

Instructors: This is a list of possible prompts to assign as a unit writing quiz.

1 Most people eat daily meals of breakfast, lunch, and dinner. What are typical daily meals in a country you know well?

2 Think of three regions in a country you know well. Explain the different types of food found in each region.

3 What three changes in diet can people make to improve their mental health?

4 What three healthy eating habits can help people lose weight?

5 What three types of food should people avoid in order to stay healthy?

NAME: ....   DATE: ....

Part A: Academic Vocabulary

Circle the correct words to complete the paragraph.

When you want to find a community-service opportunity, start by brainstorming. For example, think about how you want to **recover / provide / assist** people in your community. You could begin by
                                                                                 (1)
making a list of ideas. Then review that list and focus on your **required / primary / voluntary** concerns.
                                                                                 (2)
Focusing on the people or issues that are most important will help you commit to doing community
service. This **commitment / recovery / assistance** will make certain that you are dedicated to your
                          (3)
community service. You are more likely to become **a volunteer / an organization / a requirement**
                                                                                 (4)
when the cause is important to you. Once you have identified a cause to focus on, you can search for a
group to work with. Every community has numerous **organizations / requirements / commitments**
                                                                                 (5)
that support various people or needs in the community. To find one in your community, use the
Internet to search for groups that **assist / provide / recover** help. Some organizations have skill or age
                                                                    (6)
requirements / assistance / commitments for volunteers. Others may not ask for volunteers to have any
                (7)
experience or other qualifications. For example, the American Red Cross describes many opportunities to
help **provide / recover / require** from natural disasters, and most volunteers do not need any special skills.
              (8)
By following these steps, you will find volunteer opportunities in your community.

Part B: Academic Collocations

Complete the paragraph with the correct academic collocations in the box.

make a commitment	primary goal	provide information	meet the requirement	provide support

People interested in volunteering at the hospital should complete the following steps. First, volunteers
must .... of being 16 or older. Also, all new volunteers need to attend training.
                (1)
At this training, hospital staff will .... about volunteer responsibilities. Next, the hospital
                                                          (2)
needs each volunteer to bring a doctor's note to prove good health. The .... of the
                                                                                          (3)
hospital is to help patients have good health, so all volunteers must be healthy. Then the hospital asks all
volunteers to .... to help all patients equally, because the hospital's goal is to assist all
                  (4)
people. The final step in the volunteer process is to meet with the volunteer manager. This person will match
volunteers to their jobs and .... for volunteers who need help or have questions.
                                        (5)
After they complete these steps, people can begin volunteering at the hospital within a couple of weeks.

NAME: ....

DATE: ....

Part A

Complete the sentences with the correct form of the phrasal verbs in the box.

| count on | fill out | find out | hand out | log on | sign up |

1 The city's unemployed residents can .... the job-fair organization to help them find good jobs.

2 Yvonne successfully .... thirty job-fair volunteers who will start tomorrow.

3 This organization helps unemployed people .... what jobs are available.

4 At the job fair, volunteers .... information cards so people know who to call with questions.

5 Other volunteers show people how to .... to job-search websites.

6 Some volunteers help adults .... job applications correctly.

Part B

Replace the underlined verb in each sentence with the correct phrasal verb in the box.
Use the correct form.

| fill out | find out | sign up |

1 The food bank requires volunteers to <u>complete</u> an application before they can start work.

2 When the local high school students <u>learned</u> about the opening of the food bank, they rushed over there to help.

3 So many volunteers <u>agreed</u> to help at the food bank that the manager had to tell some to go home.

NAME: ....

DATE: ....

Part A

Four students are writing citations for online sources. What should they do in each situation?
Circle the answer.

In-text Citations

1 Kara is writing an essay on service learning. In one of her online sources, the page number is missing. What should she do in her in-text citation?

a Do not include the page number.

b Write "npn" (no page number).

2 For his paper on community-service projects in schools, Marco is using a source from a government website. However, the author's name is missing from the document. What should he do?

a Write "no author."

b Include website or article name instead of author name.

Works Cited

3 Sergei is writing a paper on recent trends in volunteerism. One of his sources doesn't list an author. How should he begin his citation in his works-cited page?

a Begin with the name of the website or the article.

b Begin with the publication date.

4 For Amanda's essay on donating blood, she found an article on a nonprofit organization's website. However, the source doesn't contain a date. How should she cite it on her works-cited page?

a Write "n.d." (no date).

b Write only the date of access.

Part B

Read each citation. Circle the letter of the unavailable information.

In-text Citations

1 According to Keith Adams, service learning can benefit those who receive the help, but it also benefits those giving it in many ways. He says that most volunteers respond so positively to service, that they usually continue to volunteer throughout their lives (Adams).

a author   b page number

2 According to the volunteersusa.org website, volunteering only a few times per year can make a difference in the lives of everyone in the community.

a date of publication   b author

Works Cited

3 Hristov, Ivan. "How Can Service-Learning Make a Change?" Peace Corps. n.d. Web. 30 April 2015.

a date of publication   b date retrieved

4 "A Call to Arts." Corporation for National and Community Service. 20 March 2015. Web. 30 April 2015.

a page number   b author

NAME: .... **DATE:** ....

Instructors: This is a list of possible prompts to assign as a unit writing quiz.

1 What steps can you take to organize a clothing drive to help homeless people in your community?

2 What is the process to find and sign up to help a volunteer organization in your community?

3 A cleanup is an event where volunteers remove garbage from a public place. What steps would you take to organize a cleanup in your neighborhood, local park, or beach?

4 Explain the steps needed to set up a community-service project at your school.

5 A fundraiser is an event to collect money for charity. What process do you need to follow to organize a fundraiser to help needy children?

NAME: ....

DATE: ....

Part A: Academic Vocabulary

Circle the correct words to complete the sentences.

1 When researching car features and prices, people can find information from hundreds of knowledgeable car **payments / experts / credits** online.

2 One **challenge / income / expert** of shopping for clothes online is that customers cannot try on the clothes before they buy them.

3 Some stores allow customers to make monthly **accounts / payments / debt** for the products they buy instead of giving them the whole amount at once.

4 In order to get a loan to buy a car, you must have enough **accounts / income / credit** from your job to pay the loan back.

5 If you return products to most stores, they usually offer either cash or **credit / payment / finance** toward another purchase.

6 Some parents open savings **experts / accounts / payments** for their children to teach them about money.

7 One way to avoid **debt / income / accounts** is to only buy what you can afford.

8 You can learn how to manage your **finances / challenges / experts** by meeting with a financial advisor.

Part B: Academic Phrases

Complete the paragraph with the academic phrases in the box.

compared to	it is clear that	such as

Buying things online is a very different shopping experience .... buying things in a
                                                                        (1)
store. For example, customers can do many things in person, ... trying on clothes or
                                                                        (2)
test driving cars, which they cannot do online. However, the online environment allows shoppers to research
all the information they need about the cost, features, and problems of a product. ....
                                                                        (3)
there are advantages and disadvantages to shopping online and in stores. For this reason, businesses should
try to offer both options to attract as many customers as possible.

NAME: ....

DATE: ....

Part A

Circle the correct comparative forms to complete the sentences.

1 Some people think buying clothing online is **more good / gooder / better** than buying it in a store because they can try on the clothes at home.

2 Some prefer buying clothing in stores because it is **convenienter / more convenienter / more convenient** than waiting for clothes to arrive in the mail.

3 Paying bills online is **faster / fast / more faster** than writing checks and mailing them.

4 With online banking, it is **easyer / more easy / easier** to check your bank balance than it used to be.

5 The price of jeans at City Discount Market is **lower / more low / low** than at Chantal's Boutique.

6 For shop owners, credit-card purchases are **expensive / more expensive / expensiver** than cash purchases. This is because they need to pay the credit company a fee.

7 Gas prices in the Midwestern U.S. are **not high / not as high as / not higher as** on the East Coast.

8 Often teens who work are **dependent / less dependent / less dependenter** on their parents for spending money than those who don't.

Part B

Correct the mistakes in the sentences.

1 Online colleges are now offering more cheap classes than traditional colleges.

2 It is more important to make sure you can afford whatever you choose to buy.

3 A credit card with a low interest rate is better that one with a high interest rate.

4 Department stores are usually busyier during sales.

5 Buying books online is becoming commoner than buying them in bookstores.

6 The interest rate at my new bank is more higher than at my old bank.

SCORE: .... / 7

NAME: ....

DATE: ....

Part A

Check (✓) the things students should do to write good paraphrases.

◻ 1 Use the same language as the original author.

◻ 2 Change the order of the words.

◻ 3 Use quotation marks.

◻ 4 Change a quote to indirect speech.

◻ 5 Change words or phrases to synonyms.

◻ 6 Change the meaning.

◻ 7 Use different word forms.

Part B

Read the quotations and paraphrases. There is a problem with each paraphrase. Circle the letter of the problem.

1 **Quotation:**

"After running up record debt-to-income ratios during the bubble economy of the 2000s, young adults shed substantially more debt than older adults did during the Great Recession and its immediate aftermath—mainly by virtue of owning fewer houses and cars, according to a new Pew Research Center analysis of Federal Reserve Board and other government data."

Source: Fry, Richard. "Young Adults After the Recession: Fewer Homes, Fewer Cars, Less Debt." *Pew Research Center.* 2 Feb 2013. Web. 4 May 2015.

Paraphrase:

According to Richard Fry in "Young Adults After the Recession: Fewer Homes, Fewer Cars, Less Debt," young adults owed more than they made in the early 2000s. After, they shed substantially more debt than older adults did during the Great Recession and its immediate aftermath—mainly by virtue of owning fewer houses and cars.

Problem:

a The writer used the original writer's exact words.

b The writer did not include the source.

2 **Quotation:**

"Second-generation Americans – the 20 million adult U.S.-born children of immigrants – are substantially better off than immigrants themselves on key measures of socioeconomic attainment, according to a new Pew Research Center analysis of U.S. Census Bureau data. They have higher incomes; more are college graduates and homeowners; and fewer live in poverty. In all of these measures, their characteristics resemble those of the full U.S. adult population."

Source: Taylor, Paul. "Second Generation Americans: A Portrait of Adult Children of Immigrants. Overview." *Pew Research Center.* 7 Feb 2013. Web. 4 May 2015.

Paraphrase:

American adults born of immigrants are better off than their parents. More of these second-generation adults have graduated from college, they own more homes, and they have higher earnings than their parents.

Problem:

a The writer used the original author's exact words.

b The writer did not include the source.

(CONTINUED)

3 **Quotation:**

"About four-in-ten U.S. households (37%) headed by an adult younger than 40 currently have some student debt – the highest share on record, with the median outstanding student debt load standing at about $13,000."

Source: Fry, Richard. "Young Adults, Student Debt and Economic Well-Being." *Pew Research Center*. 14 May 2014. Web. 30 April 2015.

Paraphrase:

According to Richard Fry of the Pew Research Center, thirty-seven percent of U.S. households have student debt of up to $13,000.

Problem:

a The writer used the original author's exact words.

b The writer changed the meaning of the original author's words.

NAME: .... **DATE:** ....

Instructors: This is a list of possible prompts to assign as a unit writing quiz.

1 The cost of college tuition, textbooks, and living expenses can differ from country to country. Compare the cost of attending college in two countries you know well.

2 Compare the price, quality, and availability of handmade goods, such as pottery, hand-sewn bags, and hand-knit hats and scarves, to factory-made items.

3 Compare buying print newspaper and magazine subscriptions with buying online subscriptions.

4 Compare the spending habits of people in two different age groups (for example, people in their teens and people in their twenties or young adults and seniors).

5 Compare the cost of living (for example, housing, food, transportation) in two cities you know well.

UNIT QUIZZES ANSWER KEY

UNIT 1

Unit 1 Vocabulary

Part A

1 master
2 critical
3 attention
4 memorize
5 sharpen
6 ability
7 technique
8 mental

Part B

1 pay attention
2 attention spans
3 learning technique
4 memory loss
5 mental health

Unit 1 Grammar

Part A

1 because
2 Although
3 since
4 While
5 even though
6 because

Part B

1 ~~Althought~~ *Although* teenagers can be moody, their behavior usually improves as they get older.

2 Reading an enjoyable book before bed is healthy~~,~~ because it relaxes you.

3 Even though Professor Lu never gives us homework on weekends to relieve our stress~~.~~' I usually study anyway.

4 I am thinking more clearly. ~~Since~~ *since* I began to do challenging crossword puzzles.

5 Although it's a good idea to avoid a lot of caffeine, ~~and~~ some people say it helps them stay alert.

Unit 1 Avoiding Plagiarism

Part A

1 b   2 a

Part B

1 Creativity, or <u>the ability to think of new ideas or make something original or innovative</u>, is used in schools. Students can learn to solve problems in a fun way, <u>not only in art classes but also in science and technology classes.</u>

2 Creativity means making new or original ideas or things. This method <u>is encouraged in schools to promote original, individual thinking</u>. Students will be able to use <u>new approaches to problem solving</u>. This is very helpful when they learn about a variety of subjects including science, technology, and the arts.

UNIT 2

Unit 2 Vocabulary

Part A

1 respectful
2 avoid
3 regard
4 interpret
5 communicate
6 custom
7 cultures
8 brief

Part B

1 a number of
2 One of the
3 Another

Unit 2 Grammar

Part A

1 some
2 few of
3 a few
4 number of
5 little
6 a large amount of

Part B

1 Most Americans try to leave ~~little~~ *a* space between themselves and strangers.

2 Today there is a large ~~number~~ *amount* of online communication across cultures.

3 Few of *the* residents of San Francisco have never been to the city's famous Chinatown.

4 People who are moving to a new country can learn about the culture by reading a lot *of* books.

5 ~~Little~~ *A little* gesture such as a smile can help people make friends in a new culture.

Unit 2 Avoiding Plagiarism

1 c   2 a   3 b

UNIT 3

Unit 3 Vocabulary

Part A

1 struggle
2 identity
3 reveal
4 social
5 concern
6 ethnic
7 acceptable
8 values

Part B

1 national identity
2 social class
3 social values
4 ethnic groups
5 ethnic background

Unit 3 Grammar

Part A

1 Chinese
2 relaxing
3 Italy
4 amazed
5 Mexican
6 interested
7 shocking
8 Australians

Part B

(1) If you are ~~interesting~~ *interested* in seeing a historic American city, I recommend you visit Boston, Massachusetts. (2) There are many ~~excite~~ *exciting* things to do, such as walking along the historic Freedom Trail, visiting the Public Garden, and taking a ride on the Swan Boats. (3) You'll find that Boston has an international flair: the South Boston neighborhood is an ~~irish~~ *Irish* neighborhood, where you'll find restaurants typical of that country. (4) If you want ~~Korea~~ *Korean* food, be sure to visit Allston Village. (5) ~~Italy~~ *Italian* food is abundant in the city's historic North End. (6) Don't be ~~confusing~~ *confused* by the city's old streets – buy a local map and you will have no trouble getting around. (7) Finally, the museums are not to be missed: the Museum of Fine Arts, the New England Aquarium, and the Museum of Science are all ~~fascinated~~ *fascinating*.

Unit 3 Avoiding Plagiarism

Part A

Check: 2, 3, 6, 7, 8

Part B

1 O	3 R	5 O	7 R
2 R	4 O	6 R	

UNIT 4

Unit 4 Vocabulary

Part A

1 control
2 policies
3 distinguish
4 habit
5 behave
6 request
7 conflict
8 encourages

Part B

1 a kind of
2 is related to
3 In other words

Unit 4 Grammar

Part A

1 A good <u>manager</u> [CS] offers <u>employees</u> [CP] a lot of <u>encouragement</u> [NC].
2 Many <u>companies</u> [CP] provide <u>information</u> [NC] about their <u>benefits</u> [CP] on an internal <u>website</u> [CS].
3 Professional <u>behavior</u> [CS] is expected at the <u>office</u> [CS], but at office <u>parties</u> [CP] <u>employees</u> [CP] can relax.
4 My <u>boss</u> [CS] is strict about <u>etiquette</u> [NC] in work-related <u>emails</u> [CP].
5 <u>Stefano</u> [CS] was happy to share his <u>knowledge</u> [NC] about the <u>organization</u> [CS] with the new <u>employee</u> [CS].
6 Open <u>communication</u> [NC] is necessary if <u>you</u> [CS] want to work well with your <u>colleagues</u> [CP].

Part B

1 encouragement
2 a good idea
3 control
4 Much
5 is
6 a colleague

Unit 4 Avoiding Plagiarism

Part A

Check: 1, 2, 5

Part B

1 b   2 a   3 b

UNIT 5

Unit 5 Vocabulary

Part A
1 concept
2 create
3 design
4 motivates
5 capable
6 explore
7 range
8 relevant

Part B
1 explore the possibility
2 basic concept
3 main motivation
4 a wide range of
5 capable of expressing

Unit 5 Grammar

Part A
1 conclusion
2 creativity
3 performance
4 happily
5 importance
6 active

Part B

(1) Parents should encourage their children to draw and paint at home because they will see the ~~differance~~ *difference* in their children's performance at school. (2) ~~Creative~~ *Creativity* can help children think clearly, therefore do better in their classes. (3) ~~Self-confidance~~ *Self-confidence* is another benefit of encouraging the arts at home because children generally feel good about their creations. (4) In addition, if they see their own artwork on display, it can be a ~~powerfull~~ *powerful* way to make them feel confident. (5) This is ~~especialy~~ *especially* true for shy children. (6) ~~Final~~, *Finally* one of the best benefits is that parents can create art along with their children. (7) This can make a big ~~different~~ *difference* in how children feel about art.

Unit 5 Avoiding Plagiarism

Part A
1 b   2 c   3 a

Part B
Check: 1, 2

UNIT 6

Unit 6 Vocabulary

Part A
1 traditional
2 contemporary
3 approach
4 medicine
5 treat
6 condition
7 eliminate
8 suffer

Part B
1 a variety of
2 it is possible
3 appears to be

Unit 6 Grammar

Part A
1 give
2 is eating
3 have
4 are eliminating
5 tastes
6 are selling
7 is thinking
8 serves

Part B
1 comes
2 are throwing
3 buy
4 toss
5 are trying
6 seem
7 is organizing
8 believe

Unit 6 Avoiding Plagiarism

Part A
1 c   2 a   3 b

Part B
1 b   2 c   3 c

UNIT 7

Unit 7 Vocabulary

Part A
1 assist
2 primary
3 commitment
4 a volunteer
5 organizations
6 provide
7 requirements
8 recover

Part B
1 meet the requirement
2 provide information
3 primary goal
4 make a commitment
5 provide support

Unit 7 Grammar

Part A

1	count on	4	hand out
2	signed up	5	log on
3	find out	6	fill out

Part B

1 The food bank requires volunteers to ~~complete~~ *fill out* an application before they can start work.
2 When the local high school students ~~learned~~ *found out* about the opening of the food bank, they rushed over there to help.
3 So many volunteers ~~agreed~~ *signed up* to help at the food bank that the manager had to tell some to go home.

Unit 7 Avoiding Plagiarism

Part A

1 a		2 b		3 a		4 a	

Part B

1 b		2 b		3 a		4 b	

UNIT 8

Unit 8 Vocabulary

Part A

1	experts	5	credit
2	challenge	6	accounts
3	payments	7	debt
4	income	8	finances

Part B

1 compared to
2 such as
3 It is clear that

Unit 8 Grammar

Part A

1	better	5	lower
2	more convenient	6	more expensive
3	faster	7	not as high as
4	easier	8	less dependent

Part B

1 Online colleges are now offering ~~more cheap~~ *cheaper* classes than traditional colleges.
2 It is ~~more~~ important to make sure you can afford whatever you choose to buy.
3 A credit card with a low interest rate is better ~~that~~ *than* one with a high interest rate.
4 Department stores are usually ~~busyier~~ *busier* during sales.
5 Buying books online is becoming ~~commoner~~ *more common* than buying them in bookstores.
6 The interest rate at my new bank is ~~more~~ higher than at my old bank.

Unit 8 Avoiding Plagiarism

Part A
Check: 2, 4, 5, 7

Part B

1 a		2 b		3 b

UNIT QUIZZES WRITING RUBRIC

Final Draft Writing Assignment Rubric

CATEGORY	CRITERIA	SCORE
Language Use	Grammar and vocabulary are accurate, appropriate, and varied. Sentence types are varied and used appropriately. Level of formality (register) shows a good understanding of audience and purpose. Mechanics (capitalization, punctuation, indentation, and spelling) are strong.	
Organization & Mode (structure)	Writing is well organized and follows the conventions of academic writing: • Paragraph – topic sentence, supporting details, concluding sentence • Essay – introduction with thesis, body paragraphs, conclusion Rhetorical mode is used correctly and appropriately. Research is clearly and correctly integrated into student writing (if applicable).	
Coherence, Clarity, & Unity	Sentences within a paragraph flow logically with appropriate transitions; paragraphs within an essay flow logically with appropriate transitions. Sentences and ideas are clear and make sense to the reader. All sentences in a paragraph relate to the topic sentence; all paragraphs in an essay relate to the thesis.	
Content & Development (meaning)	Writing completes the task and fully answers the prompt. Content is meaningful and interesting. Main points and ideas are fully developed with good support and logic.	

How well does the response meet the criteria?	Recommended Score
At least 90%	25
At least 80%	20
At least 70%	15
At least 60%	10
At least 50%	5
Less than 50%	0
Total Score Possible per Section	25
Total Score Possible	100

Feedback: